NO, I'M NOT AFRAID

Irina Ratushinskaya

No, I'm Not
AFRAID

Translated by
DAVID McDUFF

Introduction by
JOSEPH BRODSKY

BLOODAXE BOOKS

ISBN: 0 906427 95 9

First published 1986 by
Bloodaxe Books Ltd,
P.O. Box 1SN,
Newcastle upon Tyne NE99 1SN.

Bloodaxe Books Ltd acknowledges
the financial assistance of Northern Arts.

Typesetting by True North, Newcastle upon Tyne.

Printed in Great Britain by
Tyneside Free Press Workshop Ltd, Newcastle upon Tyne.

Contents

2. After the First Arrest (DECEMBER 1981 – SEPTEMBER 1982)

3. After the Second Arrest (OCTOBER 1982 – APRIL 1983)

4. Poems from the Small Zone (FROM APRIL 1983)

Acknowledgements

This selection of Irina Ratushinskaya's poetry draws on all the material currently available in the West in both published and unpublished form. As far as the dating of individual poems is concerned, every effort has been made to place each one in chronological sequence. However, there are undated poems, so that the order adopted for this book must be taken as approximate.

The translator is grateful to Yefim Kotlyar of Chicago, USA, and to Marjorie Farquharson of Amnesty International in London, for making unpublished material available to him. Thanks are also due to Joseph Brodsky, Herbert Leibowitz, Ilya Nykin, the Rev. Dr Richard Rodgers, Keston College, International P.E.N., and to P.E.N. American Center, which provided much of the information contained in the outline of Ratushinskaya's life and career.

Joseph Brodsky's Introduction first appeared in *Poems* by Irina Ratushinskaya, a trilingual edition published in 1984 by Hermitage, Ann Arbor, in association with International P.E.N. Ilya Nykin's memoir was published in *Parnassus* (vol. 11 no. 2, Fall/Winter 1983 & Spring/Summer 1984). The Amnesty International report was published in July 1985 under the title *USSR: Conditions for Women Prisoners of Conscience in the 'Small Zone'*. The extracts from *The Diary of the Small Zone* have been made from the full document, *Khronika barashevskoy (politicheskoy zhenskoy) zony*, published in *Materialy samizdata* no. 17 (20 May 1985), using a translation first published in the United States.

The Small Zone photographs (copyright Cronid Lyubarsky) and pictures of Irina Ratushinskaya (back cover and page 16), Jadvyga Bieliauskiene, Raisa Rudenko and Tatyana Velikanova are reproduced by kind permission of Amnesty International; those of Irina Ratushinskaya (pages 22 and 42), Lydia Doronina (copyright Sapiets), Galina Barats-Kokhan, Natalya Lazareva and Tatyana Osipova (copyright P. Reddaway) courtesy of Keston College; that of Lagle Parek, courtesy of *Russkaya mysl'* (Paris). Thanks are also due to International P.E.N. for supplying the front cover and frontispiece photograph of Irina Ratushinskaya.

The drawings by Irina Ratushinskaya were published on 23 August 1985 in *Materialy samizdata* no .29.

Irina Ratushinskaya

Irina Ratushinskaya has been imprisoned in a Soviet hard labour camp since April 1983. She has suffered beatings, force-feeding and solitary confinement in brutal, freezing conditions, and is now so gravely ill that she may not survive much more of her sentence. Her crime was the 'manufacture and dissemination' of her poems. Arrested for the second time in September 1982, she was charged with 'anti-Soviet agitation and propaganda' and finally sentenced in March 1983 to seven years' hard labour and five of internal exile, the maximum possible punishment for this offence.

She is said to be the youngest woman in the 'Small Zone', a special unit for women political prisoners at Barashevo in Mordovia. For her repeated protests against camp practices which flout Soviet as well as international law, Irina Ratushinskaya was transferred in August 1985 to PKT Camp No. 2 at nearby Yavas, to spend six months in an isolation cell. A report published by Radio Liberty's *Materialy samizdata* on 24 January 1986 states that on being moved to her new KGB prison, Ratushinskaya had to have her head shaved. Despite her illness (she now has a kidney disease), she was put on half rations, on a grossly inadequate bread and water diet of about 1750 calories per day. In the middle of the Russian winter, she will have been given warm food, a bowl of gruel, probably only once every two days. In these conditions she will have spent her 32nd birthday, 4th March 1986.

This book presents not just a selection of Ratushinskaya's poetry but also statements by her husband and her friends, as well as extracts from a camp diary smuggled out of the Small Zone. This extraordinary document records the experiences of a remarkable group of political prisoners, all of them women who had played an important role in the struggle for human rights and for the existence of separate nationalities within the Union of Soviet Socialist Republics.

In putting all their troublemakers into the one camp, the authorities unwittingly created a community of women who have helped sustain one another through courageous and selfless mutual support, stubbornly resisting all the infringements of penal regulations perpetrated by the camp's guards and commandant. Ratushinskaya is one of a dozen such women prisoners of conscience. In this book, through her poetry, she becomes their spokeswoman:

I will live and survive and be asked:
How they slammed my head against a trestle,
How I had to freeze at nights,
How my hair started to turn grey . . .

Irina Ratushinskaya was born in Odessa, Ukrainian SSR, on 4 March 1954. Her parents, the descendants of Russified Polish ex-gentry, who had managed to adapt to conditions of life in Russia after the Soviet takeover, brought her up in a conventional fashion, according to the strictures of Soviet cultural and political orthodoxy. Ratushinskaya's school education was also of a model Soviet kind, and she rebelled against it early on, unable to adopt the postulates and required attitudes of the Soviet "religion". Instead, she acquired a faith in Catholic Christianity, the religion of her grandparents. A lively-spirited child, she soon came into conflict with the Soviet authorities; the conflicts continued into her adolescence and adulthood.

Although she had loved literature and art from an early age, Ratushinskaya chose not to specialise in these as subjects of formal study, since in the Soviet Union most discussion of the humanities is permeated by ideological concepts and is a thoroughly risky enterprise, exposing those who participate in it to the danger of expressing political heresies which are punishable by law. Instead, she opted to study natural science. In 1976 she received a diploma degree in physics, and accepted a teaching position at the Odessa Pedagogical Institute. While at university, she had experimented with writing, mostly of a light, dramatic kind, producing scripts for humorous student revues, and a few poems. She did not begin to write in earnest until, during the late 1970s, she discovered the poetry of the Russian 'Silver Age', and that of the great 'quartet' of Russian poets, Akhmatova, Mandelstam, Pasternak and Tsvetayeva. The discovery of these poets (whom she read in the hard-to-obtain complete and semi-complete Western and Soviet editions circulating unofficially among the students) was an intense and profound spiritual experience for her, and after it she began to write her own poems with a greatly increased seriousness and sense of artistic commitment.

In 1979 she married the human rights activist Igor Gerashchenko, moved with him to Kiev, and became involved in the human rights movement after she and her husband were several times refused permission to emigrate. Ratushinskaya and Gerashchenko were interrogated on several occasions by the KGB and in August 1981 were threatened with criminal prosecution. On 10 December 1981 they were both arrested in Moscow's Pushkin Square, where they

10

had gone to take part in the traditional annual demonstration by dissidents (on this occasion it was in support of Andrei Sakharov) and were sentenced to 10 days' imprisonment, which Ratushinskaya served in Butyrki Prison. Her descriptions of this experience, together with her later article about events in Poland, were published in the underground newspaper of SMOT (Free Interprofessional Union of Workers). After being convicted, they both lost their jobs. On 17 September 1982 Ratushinskaya was arrested again. At her trial six months later the main charge against her was 'agitation carried on for the purpose of subverting or weakening the Soviet regime' (under Article 62 of the Ukrainian SSR Criminal Code). Cited in evidence was the fact that she had written and circulated poems critical of the Soviet Union.

One day after her 29th birthday, on 5 March 1983, Ratushinskaya was sentenced to seven years' hard labour (to be served in a 'strict regime' concentration camp), to be followed by five years of internal exile. The trial had lasted three days. The court had appointed the lawyer for Ratushinskaya's defence. She had not been allowed to substitute a lawyer of her own choice. She had not been permitted to conduct her own defence; she had not been allowed to complete her final testimony. Nor had her family and friends been allowed to enter the courtroom. She appealed. On 7 April two minor charges were dropped, but the major charges – that she had 'prepared and disseminated' certain poems – still stood. The sentence remained unaltered.

Five days later she was deported to the 'strict regime' camp at Barashevo, three hundred miles south-east of Moscow. In the harsh conditions of the camp, Ratushinskaya has been treated severely for being involved in many protest strikes, along with a dozen other women political prisoners. In August 1983 she went on a three-day hunger strike after being refused a visit from her husband. The visit was granted, but other hunger strikes followed. On 24 September 1983, while undergoing force-feeding with other hunger-strikers, Ratushinskaya suffered concussion. She resisted medical treatment and force-feeding in the camp, fearing the use of psychiatric drugs.

Between December 1983 and February 1984 Ratushinskaya spent a total of 39 days in an unheated punishment cell (SHIZO), where she contracted pneumonia. When her mother and mother-in-law made the long journey from Odessa to Mordovia to visit her, they were turned away at the prison gates, and she has now been denied visits from her husband for over two years.

Meanwhile her poems were being brought to the West in smuggled *samizdat* copies, cassette tape-recordings and memorised versions. They have appeared in the original Russian in such West European Russian-language journals and newspapers as *Grani, Possev, Kontinent* and *Russkaya mysl'*. In the United States, translations of her work have appeared in many of the most prominent literary journals: *Agni Review, Grand Street, The New Republic, The New York Review of Books, Parnassus: Poetry in Review, The New York Teacher, The Poet News* and *River Styx*. In Britain, her poems have appeared in *The Observer, Index on Censorship, Oxford Magazine* and *Cosmopolitan*. In 1984 a trilingual volume (in Russian, English and French) containing a short selection of her poems was published by Hermitage Press and International P.E.N., and was distributed to P.E.N. centres in thirty countries around the world. Public readings of her work have been given in New York and Los Angeles, and Representative John Porter has made a speech on her behalf on the floor of the U.S. Congress.

Most recent reports, including one from Igor Gerashchenko, state that Ratushinskaya is still being held in solitary confinement. She is suffering from kidney trouble and high blood pressure, and is receiving no treatment for either of these. She is permitted only five books in her cell, which must be officially-approved Russian classics, and is not permitted to write.

In April 1985 Gerashchenko addressed an impassioned appeal to 'all European Parliamentarians' to raise their voices in protest at the treatment of his wife. He asked for their help in the name of their mothers and of women everywhere, and attacked the indifference of people who remained silent because they were afraid of angering the powerful Soviets. Ratushinskaya's sentence was, he said, 'based on five poems as remote from politics as the Lord's Prayer'.

Concern for Ratushinskaya in the West has grown following the death of another young prisoner of conscience, Valery Marchenko, from a kidney condition similar to hers. Stepped-up efforts on her behalf have included letters and cables from P.E.N. American Center to Soviet and American officials, and a letter to Jesse Jackson asking him to plead for her on any trip he might make to the Soviet Union.

At their conference in New York in January 1986, International P.E.N. called for the release of Irina Ratushinskaya and other jailed Russian writers. In November 1984 P.E.N. had appealed to the Soviet authorities to invoke their own law for the remission of Ratushinskaya's sentence. Under Article 100 of the RSFSR Penal Code, the remainder of a prisoner's sentence can be remitted if he is too ill to serve it, and P.E.N. have suggested that letters politely citing this possibility could be sent to Mikhail Gorbachev. In the latest demonstration of support for Ratushinskaya, a priest working for Keston College, the Rev. Dr Richard Rodgers, staged a protest during February and March 1986 in the middle of Birmingham to draw the British public's attention to her plight. With his head shaved, he spent the whole of Lent in conditions similar to hers, living in a cage on bread and water prison rations for 46 days. Irina Ratushinskaya was imprisoned for her poetry. Could her poetry now secure her freedom? If it is powerful enough to move people to act on her behalf, perhaps it can.

ADDRESSES:

Mikhail Gorbachev	General Secretary of TsK KPSS, M.S. Gorbachevu, Moskva, Kreml, USSR.
Irina Ratushinskaya	431200 Mordovian ASSR, Tengushevsky Raion, Pos. Yavas, Uchr. ZhKh 385/3-2, Ratushinskaya Irina, USSR.
Igor Gerashchenko	g. Kiev, Prospekt Vernadskogo 85/59, Gerashchenko Igor, USSR.

Introduction by JOSEPH BRODSKY

Irina Ratushinskaya, the author of this collection of poems, is currently in Mordovia serving the fourth year of her seven-year term in a 'strict regime camp'. Within the judicial system, this terminology serves to obfuscate the phenomenon of penal servitude. Upon her discharge from the camp, Ratushinskaya is faced with five years of internal exile, which means that, arrested at 28, the poet will gain her liberty at 40. By implementing the time of its subjects in such a fashion, the state, to all appearances, is seeking to guarantee itself a future.

This collection contains, among others, the poems, whose 'manufacture and dissemination' brought down upon the 28-year-old writer the state's wrath, which manifested itself in such an inhuman sentence. No matter what ratio it established between the genuineness of art and the fate of its creator, the state consistently overlooks the fact that a crown of thorns on the head of a bard has a way of turning into a laurel. Any art, and especially poetic art, which has to do with language, is always simultaneously older and longer-lasting than the state. The manufacture of verse is more ineluctable than a socialist − or, for that matter, than any political system; and its dissemination also transcends the boundaries laid down for the state by space and time. Hence the state's fear and hatred of a genuine poet, its jealousy and hatred for that which will outlive it.

To hide a poet behind bars is like breaking a watch, it is a falsification of time, for poetic metre is nothing other than restructured time. What's referred to as the music of poetry, what's regarded as the poet's lyricism, is the fusion of time and language, the illumination of language by time. Ratushinskaya is a remarkably genuine poet, a poet with faultless pitch, who hears historical and absolute time with equal precision. She's a full-fledged poet, natural, with a voice of her own, piercing but devoid of hysteria. This is not the proper place for discussing her literary genealogy, although her work reveals the influence of Tsvetayeva and Akhmatova. And yet the poet, as well as the reader, should be grateful to fate for the presence of such influences. Whatever bad luck Russia may have had in this century, it has been extraordinarily lucky with its poetry. Ratushinskaya's poems confirm the fact that the luck holds. The price of this luck, however, has been frightful, as is confirmed by her fate.

A political judicial system is criminal in and of itself; the very conviction of a poet is not only a criminal offence but above all an anthropological one, for it constitutes an offence against language, against that which differentiates man from beast. Toward the end of the second millennium after the birth of Christ, the conviction of a 28-year-old woman for the manufacture and dissemination of poems whose content was unsuitable to the state strikes one as a Neanderthal shriek; or rather, it testifies to the degree of bestialisation achieved by the first socialist state in the history of mankind.

About the Arrest of Irina Ratushinskaya
by IGOR GERASHCHENKO

I have written the text of this press interview with Western correspondents in advance, conscious that the likelihood of my being able to hold a live press conference is not very great – not because the readers (and, consequently, the correspondents) of the newspapers of the free world are not interested in the fate of prisoners of conscience in the USSR, but because the Soviet authorities are doing everything in their power to see to it that such press conferences should not take place.

I have already attempted to visit Moscow and meet correspondents there. The militia arrested me as I was about to board the train and released me a few hours later, explaining that they had acted on the instructions of the KGB.

I shall make a further attempt to get through to Moscow, but am transmitting this written interview in case I am deprived of freedom for more than just a few hours.

To start with, I shall give some brief biographical information about **Irina Ratushinskaya**, and then reply to the questions which I think would be asked me at any press conference.

So: **Irina Ratushinskaya** was born in Odessa on 4 March 1954 into a family of Polish gentry which by a miracle managed to survive the Soviet takeover and adapted well to the new social order. To be on the safe side, her parents registered as Russian nationals, and indeed in both their personal documents and in their way of life they strove to present themselves as Russians – life is easier in the USSR that way.

Irina's childhood and school years were very difficult. It is evident that from birth she found the psychology of Soviet man and the Soviet religion unacceptable to her. Every attempt – whether by her parents or by her school – to make a builder of communism out of her led to conflicts; but in so far as Irina did well at school these conflicts did not go too far.

Irina started to believe in God at an early age and it was this faith – not her atheistic family upbringing and school education – which formed and preserved her soul.

In 1971 she began her studies at the University of Odessa. Her student years passed easily and happily. Starting in her first year, Irina began to earn her own living, and this end to the financial dependence on her parents she had previously known made life easier for her.

In the Faculty of Physics where she studied there were still the remnants of the Khrushchev-era 'thaw'; the students were not too much in the shadow of the departments of Communist Party History or other communist studies. And in any case, physics and mathematics are relatively unaffected by party doctrine, even in the USSR.

A university fashion of those years were the so-called KVNs (humorous theatrical competitions involving two teams), and Irina soon became one of the principal scriptwriters for the KVN team of her faculty.

In 1976 these clement student years came to an end and Irina began employment, first as a schoolteacher of physics and mathematics, and then as an assistant lecturer at the Odessa Pedagogical Institute.

Irina was involved in clashes with the authorities early on.

In 1972 the KGB attempted to recruit her as an informer; receiving a decisive refusal, the organisation spent a long time making threatening noises, but on that occasion the matter went no further.

In 1977 one of the Odessa theatres staged the première of a show of which Irina was one of the scriptwriters. After this première the show was taken off and all those who had taken part in it were hauled off for a lengthy visit to the KGB, who had detected what they considered to be 'anti-Soviet attitudes' in it. In the same year, while Irina was still working in the Pedagogical Institute, she was offered a post on the examination committee; it was explained to her that special requirements were to be made in the case of Jewish school-leavers. Irina declined the position, and in punishment for this was transferred to the laboratory staff; shortly after that, she was forced to give up her employment altogether.

Irina began to write poems at an early age – at first these were really not much more than jokes, and she did not take them seriously. It was not until around 1977 that she realised poetry was her vocation.

In 1979 Irina became my wife and moved to Kiev. The Soviet way of life was equally unacceptable to both Irina and myself, and we decided to leave the USSR. In 1980 we applied for external passports which would entitle us to travel abroad. Even though the right to exit from our country is guaranteed by Soviet law, we were refused visas. The refusal was made unofficially, our attention being drawn to the fact that it is only Jews who are permitted to leave the Soviet Union. There is no doubt in my mind that even if we had been Jews, then the

18

authorities would have refused us on some other pretext, or without any pretext at all – the answer would have been 'no', and that is all there would have been to it. For a totalitarian regime the observation of human rights is a far more terrible thing than the threat of nuclear war.

We did not and do not belong to those Soviet citizens whose numerous demands are made the pretext for the persecution of dissidents in the USSR, and we did not consider it possible to conceal this. The first human rights letter we wrote was addressed to the Soviet Government and dealt with the unlawful exile of Academician Sakharov.

In August 1981 Irina and I were summoned to the offices of the KGB, where we were threatened with arrest if we did not give up our activities on behalf of human rights. The KGB demanded that Irina stop writing poetry.

Shortly after this, the repression started. On 5 November 1981, I was sacked from my job, and it was thereafter made impossible for me to work in my special field. Our family was deprived of the means of subsistence, and there is no unemployment benefit in the USSR. We earned a living as best we could: we carried out repairs in the apartments of friends, and I managed to make a little money doing light metal work.

On 10 December 1981, during the annual demonstration in defence of human rights in Moscow's Pushkin Square, Irina and I were arrested. We had gone to the square in the company of the American correspondent Bob Gillette.

We were each given 10-day jail sentences. Irina served her first term in Butyrki Prison.

When in August 1982 we were offered farm-labouring work for the duration of the apple harvest, we leapt at the chance. It was only later, after Irina's arrest, that I discovered that this offer of work came from the KGB. This work of ours was very convenient for the KGB: we were part of a brigade of *shabashniki* (seasonal workers), from whom they planned to extort the necessary incriminating testimony under duress (i.e. the threat that they would not be paid for the work they had done).

Irina was arrested on the morning of 17 September 1982 and was taken off in handcuffs to the Investigatory Prison of the KGB – the same prison in which prisoners of the Gestapo were tortured by the Nazis during the wartime occupation of Kiev.

I have said nothing of the reason for Irina's arrest – I shall say nothing about her poems here, as that would be superfluous: let those who wish to read them do so. I shall restrict myself to one small piece of bibliographical information: a collection of Ratushinskaya's poems has been published by the firm of Possev; there is a small selection of her poems in the journal *Grani* (No. 123) – these are for the Western reader. For the Soviet reader, there are Ratushinskaya's *Poems*, which are available only in a clandestine *samizdat* publication.

QUESTION: What happened to your wife?

REPLY: Irina was arrested on the morning of 17 September in the village of Lyshnya, not far from Kiev, where we were working on the apple harvest. She was handcuffed and taken away to the investigatory prison of the KGB. On the evening of the same day it became known that she was being accused of an especially serious State crime: the writing of poems.

QUESTION: Was your wife's arrest unexpected?

REPLY: Both yes and no. No – because Irina had been writing poems without submitting them to the censors for a long time, and it is well-known that in the USSR this kind of activity is especially dangerous (for those who practise it). And if literary works circulate in *samizdat* and are published abroad, their author already has one foot in prison. Moreover, on 15 August 1981, a year before her arrest, Irina had been summoned to KGB headquarters and warned that her poems were a threat to the security of the Soviet Union, since they constituted an undermining of the Soviet regime, and that the Soviet regime had no option but to defend itself against them. We were well aware, of course, how the Soviet regime defends itself against its own citizens (by then we had read *The Gulag Archipelago*). And yes – because an arrest is always something unexpected.

QUESTION: Had you hoped for a less dismal future than the one you were faced with?

REPLY: Of course we had. We had wanted to emigrate to the USA.

QUESTION: Why did you want to leave the USSR?

REPLY: It was just a simple desire to escape from the concentration camp in which we had somehow found ourselves born.

QUESTION: Tell me, has Irina Ratushinskaya ever called for the overthrow of the Soviet regime?

REPLY: No. Irina's poetry is an expression of her attitude towards God and the world in which she lives; her poems are remote from politics. In order to call for the overthrow of a regime one must have some idea of what one wishes to replace it with. For Irina herself, the most suitable social structure would be democracy on the Western model – but she has always been quite clear in her mind that such a structure would not suit the overwhelming majority of people in the Soviet Union.

QUESTION: Do you share the opinion of the KGB that your wife's poems constitute a threat to the Soviet regime?
REPLY: Yes, because they do. To a regime that is founded on a lie, any work of art is dangerous.

QUESTION: In that case it would not be in the interests of the regime to let your wife go to the West, where she would be able to write and publish her poems. In prison she will not be able to do that.
REPLY: That's not quite correct. Poems are created in the soul, not on paper. I would find it difficult to say which is the best environment for poetic creation – the West, where people have enough to eat, or the concentration camp, where everyone goes hungry. As regards publication, the experience of recent years shows that prison walls in the USSR can be penetrated both by poetry and by prose.

QUESTION: What can you tell us about the conduct of Irina's trial?
REPLY: Irina's arrest was preceded by four searches of our own apartment and four searches of the apartments of our friends. But the KGB were very unlucky – they did not succeed in discovering documents, the possession of which would lead to imprisonment under Soviet law. It is also impossible to treat Irina's poems as anti-Soviet agitation and propaganda, even according to Soviet law. The preliminary interrogations of her friends and relatives likewise yielded no results – 15 people refused to make depositions. The KGB had no material evidence relating to the case. But the KGB is not the sort of organisation to close a political case because of the absence of material evidence. Since Irina had been arrested, material evidence had to be acquired by whatever means possible. Mass interrogations (both formal and informal) were begun, accompanied by threats, blackmail and promises of help in exchange for compliancy. People who had never known Irina, but had merely seen her on one or two occasions, were interrogated. During the interrogation of witnesses the KGB *never once* told them what the concrete nature of Irina's offence was – this was in complete infringement of Soviet law. What in essence the KGB tried to do was to use the witnesses as informers, demanding answers to all questions that were of interest to them, irrespectively of whether these had any relevance to the Ratushin-

21

skaya case or not. If the person under interrogation refused to play the sickening role of informer, he or she would be threatened with criminal proceedings. At the present time I know of 75 such interrogations, but assume that their number is significantly greater.

None of the people who really knew Irina gave evidence to the court, so that the KGB would have to use fake witnesses and find her guilty of an 'unenthusiastic way of thinking'.

Irina Ratushinskaya with Igor Gerashchenko.

Irina Ratushinskaya: a memoir by ILYA NYKIN

I first met her on the campus of the University of Odessa, where I studied maths and computer science. With a bunch of fellow students we were labouring over a script for a comedy show. It was almost exactly ten years ago, in an auditorium of the Main Building – enter from Peter the Great Street, up the stairs to the third floor, turn left.

By that time it was already clear that my own literary talents were of a somewhat limited magnitude. So I usually served as the editor-in-chief (an arrangement not very uncommon, as I now understand). Editing and pasting the text of our collective masterpiece, I noticed that all the best lines originated from one source, who turned out to be a young, very slender girl of about five feet seven. She looked a bit like Mary from Peter, Paul and Mary, only her straight hair was brown.

Her name was Irina Ratushinskaya. She attended the School of Physics. Though not the most beautiful girl in her class, she was easily the most popular. And that was all I knew about her for a while.

It wasn't until two-and-a-half years later that she showed me one of her poems. The poem was about aeroplanes. Irina had dreamed of flying one for a long time, but her application for a pilot's licence was rejected because of a weak reflex in some obscure ankle muscle. I've never heard of any such reflex, and for all I know the Union of Soviet Socialist Republics could be the only place on Earth where they check for it. At any rate, they wouldn't let her fly, so she wrote something of a love letter addressed to 'my aeroplanes'.

In elementary school we were taught that the aeroplane had been invented by a Russian engineer. Neither Irina nor I remembered the man's name, but to the best of our recollection he was not the same Russian engineer who had invented the radio and the telegraph. We spent the rest of the afternoon sharing other observations related to Soviet education. Then I bought two ice-cream cones and we rushed to the cinema around the corner.

Irina's poems of the seventies were crisp, mischievous, and romantic. She certainly defied the stereotype – that of a poet who spends long hours at home, preferably in a half-lit room, searching for metaphors and being otherwise unhappy. In fact, it was awfully hard to catch her at home at all. She couldn't stand small rooms, lifts, and narrow corridors. She was always outdoors. Her schedule was packed with hiking trips. She was always camping some place or other. She had a reputation as a first rate ping-pong player, beating her male and female opponents alike. She was an excellent swimmer and could easily swim a couple of miles off shore, leaving her more timid friends behind.

She liked to take long brisk walks through the winter city streets. Never mind the wind from the sea! We talked about witchcraft and gypsies and God knows how many other important things. In the evening we would sit in my study and drink Turkish coffee. I would read her some Osip Mandelstam, and she would treat me to a lesson in ancient Russian history.

So it didn't come as a complete surprise to find out after a while that Irina was the descendant of a very old Russian family. Two junior branches of that family, *Golitziny* and *Kuraginy*, had been among top figures of the Court for centuries. Perhaps even more significant was another part of her heritage – a Polish family active in the revolts against occupation by the Russian Empire. What many of us learned about Poland during the days of Solidarity, Irina, I think, had known all along.

With time her poems became more reserved. She spent longer hours writing, and for the first time she appeared to take seriously her drawings and watercolours (skilful and elegant, they were the subject of our admiration for years). Somehow she felt that time was running out, and without a hint of melodrama, almost in passing, she could mention that to a friend. She didn't know why, or at least she wasn't sure. It wasn't anything that she had done or intended to do. It could have been a shadow of precognition. It could have been a sense of destiny.

If you want a sure bet, bet that the life of a talented Russian poet will be tragic. In this century alone you would have won many a time. Irina was not a political activist. She didn't choose poetry for a weapon of struggle – whatever that means. She was just too talented. And she was also too loyal to her friends. And she wouldn't relinquish her right to honesty even when writing about her country. So, as the typed copies of her unpublished poems were passed from hand to hand, she was arrested and charged with 'anti-Soviet agitation and propaganda'.

Her offence was considered criminal rather than political, for of course there can be no political offenders in the land of victorious socialism. Her trial lasted three days. She was not allowed to substitute a lawyer of her choice for the court-appointed defender. She was not allowed to represent herself either. She was not allowed to finish her final testimony. Her family members and friends were not allowed inside the courtroom, which was filled with workers from a nearby plant. A day after her 29th birthday she was sentenced to seven years of hard labour followed by five years of internal exile. The black book of GULAG trivia will record her as the first woman to receive the maximum sentence allocated for this particularly dangerous crime. We will probably still be arguing whether the moral of *1984* applies to "us" or to "them" when "they" release Irina in 1995 (if they do).

Her first hunger strike came when she and other women in her camp were required to wear a special sign on their camp uniforms. The Soviet Special Prosecutor at the Nuremberg trials of Nazi war criminals spoke passionately of how signs of this kind 'humiliate human dignity'. Perhaps this outdated notion doesn't apply to poets and other individuals who stand in the way of progress.

Punishment must be cruel and unusual, or else why bother? The selfless workers of justice who run her labour camp are pretty damned good in getting this point across. For example, over the years, freezing punishment cells have proven to be an excellent means of criminal rehabilitation. The guards can put her in the cell for whatever reason they see fit. They can keep her in the cell for as long as they deem appropriate. And they can put her back if she still isn't catching on.

The last time she stayed in the cell for almost two months. She contracted pneumonia there. She wasn't treated, and she still suffers from severe complications. Apparently because of that her latest appointment with her husband Igor had been cancelled. The previous one had been cancelled too. Her censored letters (two a month) somehow tend to disappear 'in the mail'.

I wonder whether you find all this a bit too depressing. I wonder whether in the past few minutes the SO-WHAT-CAN-I-DO thought has crossed your mind. If it did, may I tell you of a scene from a comedy show I once saw?

It wasn't unlike some of the things we produced ten years ago at the University of Odessa. It lasted no long than half a minute. At first the stage was dark. Then a flashlight beam landed on the scared face of a mime, who said: 'What can I do alone, anyway?' Another beam, another mime: 'What can I do alone, anyway?' There were about twenty of them on that stage. Their faces appeared out of the darkness one by one, and each of them said: 'What can I do alone, anyway?' They marched away backstage, chanting all together, their voices almost cheerful: 'What can I do alone, anyway? What can I do alone anyway? What can I do alone, anyway? What can I do alone, anyway?'

I don't know who wrote this. Not Irina, although it does resemble some of her brilliant little dramas.

But this is beside the point.

[1984]

'The Calling of a Poet is to Speak the Truth'

The following comment on the arrest of Irina Ratushinskaya was recorded on to tape by one of her friends. In Russia it is secretly distributed by means of magnitizdat, *together with her poems and songs.*

During the last months Irina lived in the constant expectation of arrest. It seems that it was precisely this state of mind that helped her to write. The main thing to stress is that she was not afraid. Even though she could write the lines: 'It isn't true, I *am* afraid, my darling! / But make it look as though you haven't noticed,' she was not afraid in the direct sense of the word. She suffered from worry, from a sense of total defencelessness. But Irina had too much of a sense of her own worth and too great a contempt for danger to be really afraid. Completely unsuited to any kind of underground existence, a poet to the marrow of her bones, she constantly felt the need to make her way in the outside world, not only in the figurative sense but also literally. Irina was mortally weary, she wanted to leave Russia. But the authorities would not let her. They had selected their victim.

There are some arrests which we, grown accustomed to constant searches and investigations, perceive as being almost something that is right and proper, as something that is a matter of course. Irina's arrest does not belong in this category. It is a tragedy. A tragedy not only for us, her friends – but for Russian poetry. A poet with a vision of the world that is startling, unique in its tenacity and its penetration of colours and sounds, is behind bars. Gumilyov, Mandelstam, Brodsky, Natalya Gorbanevskaya, and now – Irina Ratushinskaya. For more than 60 years now our poetry has been shot in the back in this fashion, and we have looked on helplessly. What more can we do? Shout? We are shouting.

The arrest of Ratushinskaya is such a cynical and perverted act that right up to the last moment I was unable to believe that the government would take this step. I had to believe it. What can one say about a government that is forced to kill poets in order to maintain law and order? Why is our poetry time and time again the subject of such frenzied attacks? A true poet cannot lie. To be silent, or to be reluctant to see the world in which one lives in its true colours – that is also a lie! The calling of a poet is to speak the truth, even though it may be a subjective truth. Yet even that subjective, feminine truth is apparently considered by the government to be a danger to the State.

I will not raise the question of what kind of a State this is, which must crazily defend itself against a woman. We know the answer to that question from our own experience. No matter how dreadful it may be to say it, I believe that for a poet in our country to be arrested is a compliment. A peculiar form of recognition for his services to the motherland. The services Irina Ratushinskaya has rendered have certainly received recognition.

THE SMALL ZONE

PLAN OF THE SMALL ZONE

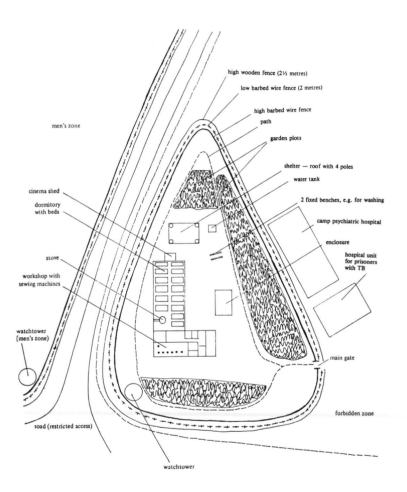

high wooden fence (2½ metres)

low barbed wire fence (2 metres)

high barbed wire fence

path

garden plots

men's zone

shelter — roof with 4 poles

water tank

cinema shed

2 fixed benches, e.g. for washing

dormitory
with beds

camp psychiatric hospital

enclosure

hospital unit
for prisoners
with TB

stove

workshop with
sewing machines

watchtower
(men's zone)

main gate

forbidden zone

road (restricted access)

watchtower

Russian Women Prisoners of Conscience

A report by Amnesty International on the Small Zone of Mordovian corrective labour colony No. 3

1. CAMP CONDITIONS

The network of corrective labour colonies called 'Dubrovlag' ('The Oak Leaf Camps') was built during the Stalin era in the Mordovian Autonomous Republic, about 450 kilometres south-east of Moscow. It consists of at least 14 labour colonies stretching north of the main Moscow-Saransk railway line and administered centrally from the town of Yavas. Each colony within the complex bears the Dubrovlag code – ZhKh 385 – followed by its own number.

The Dubrovlag includes the only known labour camp in the USSR for women who are 'especially dangerous state criminals'. This is Zone 4 of corrective labour colony number 3 at Barashevo, one of about six zones that make up that colony. Inmates call this the 'Small Zone'. At present ten women are held in Zone 4 whom Amnesty International regards as prisoners of conscience, since they are imprisoned solely for the non-violent exercise of their right to freedom of expression. The purpose of this paper is to describe the conditions of their imprisonment. Brief biographies appear in section two of the paper.

The prisoners in ZhKh 385/3-4 are kept on a 'strict regime', which is the harshest regime of imprisonment allowed for women under Soviet law. Over the years information about the zone has become available from a variety of sources. Sometimes brief reports have appeared in unofficial human rights publications, such as *A Chronicle of Current Events*, which has been compiled in Moscow since 1968. Friends and relatives of inmates have also described their visits to Zone 4 and in some cases former prisoners of conscience have written about their imprisonment, or have emigrated and spoken about it in detail. From all these materials it has been possible to build up a description of the camp.

In early 1985 there appeared abroad through unofficial channels a 23-page diary, which had reportedly been compiled secretly by inmates of Zone 4 and which gives the most up-to-date account of life in the camp. The information recorded in the diary is consistent with various other reports which Amnesty International has received about life in Zone 4 and the organisation believes that it is authentic.

The basic layout of ZhKh 385/3-4 can be seen in the diagram on page 30. The Small Zone is tucked into the corner of a much larger camp for ordinary women criminal prisoners. It is only about 60 square metres in area and consists of one large building, three strips of garden, and two outdoor laundry troughs. The building has accommodation for twenty women – although during the early 1970s it was overcrowded – and houses a dormitory, kitchen, dining room (with television), sewing shop and store room. In 1978 a radiator system replaced an old wood-burning stove.

Throughout the year inmates of the camp wear a short-sleeved striped dress of dark grey, or dark brown cotton; a plain cotton headscarf; thick stockings; and heavy black boots. Slippers are permitted only in the living quarters and outside working hours. In cold weather the women are given a short quilted jacket of black cotton, without a collar. On the chest and sleeve of their uniform all the prisoners must wear an identity label ('*birka*'), which gives their name, length of sentence, and the article of the criminal code under which they were sentenced. Many of the women have complained that the wearing of this label is one of the most humiliating aspects of life in the zone, and according to the compilers of the *samizdat* diary, it has been a continual source of friction between the prisoners and the administration.

Reveille is at 6 a.m. The women begin work at 8 a.m., have an evening meal at 7 p.m. and the lights are put out at 10 p.m. They work eight hours a day and six days a week making gloves. The noise of the machines in the confined work space is reported to be very stressful, and prisoners are not allowed to move from their sewing machines during work hours. Over the years the women's daily output target has risen. In 1978 it was 60 pairs of gloves, and in early 1984 it was reported to be 70 pairs. For meeting their target prisoners are paid five roubles

Corner sentry post of the Small Zone.

32

a month. If they produce more than their quota they can buy seven roubles' worth of goods from the camp shop each month. The shop opens twice a month and sells white bread, margarine, poor quality caramel, pens, exercise books, envelopes and stamps, combs and toiletries. The women are punished if they fail to go to work, or if they do not meet their production target.

The prisoners get three meals a day, but their diet is montonous and vitamin-deficient. Breakfast and lunch are usually *kasha* (a porridge made from oats or barley), or noodles with a small quantity of butter. The evening meal is soup made from cabbage, pork, or fish – but reportedly

View of the camp "street" running down the wooden fence of the women's camp. On the right are steps leading up to the corner sentry post.

the ingredients are often decaying or dirty. Each meal is served with black bread which has not always been properly baked and sometimes contains objects like string. In early 1983 the women ate grasses and herbs from the garden plots mixed with sunflower oil to supplement their diet, but in August 1983 the head of Zone 4 reportedly dug up their gardens. The prisoners have commonly complained that their food is too salty: the compilers of the diary, for instance, claim that each woman receives a salt ration of 25 grams a day which is added to her food regardless of taste. There are no special meals for women with health problems, like the Ukrainian prisoner of conscience Raisa Rudenko, who for ten years before her arrest was placed on a strictly controlled diet with limitation on salt, fish and meat. To improve their diet inmates of Zone 4 have asked for permission to prepare their own food, but they have so far been refused.

Like all prisoners in the Soviet corrective labour system, the women in ZhKh 385/3-4 face a variety of punishments for failing to meet their work targets, or for other alleged infringements of the regulations. They may lose their shopping privileges, or their rights to visits and correspondence may be cancelled. (Prisoners on a strict regime are entitled to receive three visits a year and to write two letters a month). For more serious offences, such as holding collective protests, or insulting the administration, prisoners may be punished by confinement in a cell. Judging from the *samizdat* diary, some prisoners of conscience have been put in cells repeatedly, without regard to their state of health.

The punishment apparently most feared by inmates of Zone 4 is SHIZO, which is detention for up to 15 days in a special punishment and isolation cell. The SHIZO block is in Zone 2 of corrective labour colony No.3. Each cell in the block is small and has four beds at two levels, like the beds in a railway sleeping car. During the day all four are raised and locked shut to the wall. In between them is a low table and four small chairs. A heavy slop pail is chained to one wall in the corner, and there is a radiator which reportedly rarely works. The prisoners are deprived of any stimulus which would help them pass the time: they are not allowed to take pen, paper, books, cigarettes or toiletries in with them. The prisoners of conscience from Zone 4 are not even taken out of the SHIZO cell to work, in case they mix with criminal prisoners from other zones.

The worst feature of SHIZO, however, is the intense cold, according to women who have experienced this punishment. The cell has a wooden floor with gaps between its boards, and underneath, a layer of solid cement, said to be about 40-50 centimetres thick. The window has bars but often no glass. In SHIZO the prisoners receive food rations only on alternate days. On the "empty" day, they are given just bread and a hot drink three times. Light bedding is handed out to them at night and taken away again in the morning, so there is nothing they can use to keep warm. According to regulations the temperature in SHIZO should not drop below 16° centigrade, but prisoners have

The staff headquarters, with a column of women prisoners being marched outside.

34

measured temperatures as low as 8° with thermometers smuggled into the cell, and reported snow lying on the inside window ledge. The SHIZO uniform intensifies the cold. The women must wear slippers and a thin dress, and hand over their stockings, headscarf and normal dress. In February 1984 a new rule forbade them to wear an underskirt in SHIZO, but the compilers of the *samizdat* diary report that this provoked such strong protest that it was not enforced. The slippers are used by all the prisoners who are put in SHIZO (colony No.3 is said to have around 2000 inmates) and the risk of foot infections is high.

Another punishment is detention for between one and six months in the corrective labour colony's internal prison – or PKT from its Russian initials. The cell is the same as the SHIZO cell, but the regime is less harsh. Inmates are given bedding during the day and warmer clothes, and are allowed out for half an hour's daily exercise. The diet is better than in SHIZO and the women are allowed to smoke and read. They can also buy two roubles' worth of goods from the camp shop. In one case a prisoner of conscience from Zone 4 was punished by eight days' solitary detention in a cell for psychiatric patients, but this appears to have been an isolated punishment. **Irina Ratushin-skaya** was put in the so-called "psychiatric box" in March 1984 while she was on a hunger-strike, and kept in conditions which reportedly fell below standards for the humane treatment of prisoners laid down by the International Covenant on Civil and Political Rights. The cell had no natural light or ventilation, and Ratushinskaya was not taken out for exercise thoughout the eight days.

Many inmates of ZhKh 385/3-4 have reported that poor diet and repeated punishments in SHIZO and PKT have damaged their health. Heart and liver diseases have been reported, as well as skin diseases, kidney pains and cystitis. There is no medical unit within the zone, and no telephone for emergencies. A nurse visits the women once a day and a doctor comes once a week, but the treatment available is said to be rudimentary and difficult to obtain outside their rounds. The hospital is in Zone 2 of ZhKh 385/3 and serves several thousand prisoners, so is often too crowded to take new patients. The doctor has wide powers to improve the prisoners' conditions, if she chooses to exercise them. For example, she can exempt them from spells in SHIZO or PKT, if she rules them unfit for the punishment. She can also let them off work on grounds of ill health when they are on hunger-strike. According to the women who compiled the *samizdat* diary, however, the doctor of Zone 4 has consistently placed the wishes of the administration before the needs of her patients. For instance, on December 1983 the prisoner of conscience Tatyana Osipova was certified fit to spend 15 days in SHIZO only minutes after she had been prescribed five days' treatment for pyelonephritis.

Like other prisoners in the Soviet corrective labour system, the inmates of ZhKh 385/3-4 have limited scope to complain about their treatment, or get redress if their rights are violated.They have no access to a lawyer, and the complaints they send out of the zone are read, and often confiscated, by the officials they are complaining about. Formally the women can send uncensored complaints to the Procuracy, which is responsible for ensuring that their legal rights are observed. In practice, however, the Procuracy has often turned their letters over for investigation by officials in the zone. When a Procurator visited Zone 4 in January 1984, the authors of the *samizdat* diary note that this was his first appearance in years. (Some inmates had by that time been in the zone for nearly three years.)

As a protest of last resort, many prisoners have refused to go to work, or have declared hunger-strikes, which are themselves punishable offences. Between late 1983 and late 1984 the prisoners of conscience in ZhKh 385/3-4 are reported to have fasted for a total of 203 days. Most of their hunger-strikes were on behalf of women who had had their visits cancelled or who had been put in SHIZO without receiving a thorough medical examination first.

The barbed wire "web". Behind it a fence is visible with "signal" wire stretched above.

The camp gates. On the right is a notice to drivers.

2. THE WOMEN PRISONERS OF CONSCIENCE

All ten of the prisoners of conscience currently in ZhKh 385/3-4 were convicted of 'anti-Soviet agitation and propaganda', a charge which is officially classified as 'an especially dangerous crime against the state' and carries a maximum sentence of seven years' imprisonment followed by five years' internal exile. Formally the law punishes 'subversion' against the state, but in hundreds of cases Soviet courts have applied it solely to punish individuals who have expressed views, or possessed or distributed material, disapproved of by the authorities. Amnesty International believes the women listed below are imprisoned for the non-violent exercise of the right to freedom of expression which is guaranteed in Article 19 of the International Covenant on Civil and Political Rights. It is appealing to the Soviet authorities for their immediate, unconditional release.

Two of the women come from the Lithuanian republic. **Edita Abrutiene** received permission to emigrate to the USA with her family in 1979. Months later, her husband was arrested and imprisoned for 'circulating anti-Soviet slander'. Abrutiene campaigned actively for his release, and in December 1982 she was herself arrested in Vilnius and accused of speaking with foreign journalists and sending information abroad about her husband's case. Edita Abrutiene was sentenced to four years' imprisonment and two years' internal exile, a term she is due to complete in December 1988. She is believed to be in her thirties. Details of her health are not known.

Jadvyga Bieliauskiene, a 55-year-old school teacher, is serving four years' imprisonment followed by three years' internal exile. She was arrested in October 1982 after officials searched her home in Kaunas district and confiscated eight books on Lithuanian history, notes by prisoners on their conditions of imprisonment, and the text of a speech given by a Lithuanian prisoner of conscience at his trial. She is due to be released in October 1989. Bieliauskiene is married and was imprisoned for eight years during the Stalin era for her involvement with

Lithuanian partisans who resisted post-war unification with the USSR. Other inmates of the Small Zone have expressed concern about her health. She has had a history of tuberculosis and reportedly suffers from liver disease, pyelonephritis and stenocardia. In 1972 her gall bladder was removed.

Galina Barats-Kokhan, now 39, was a lecturer in Marxism at Moscow University until she became a member of the Pentecostalist Church and in 1977 applied to emigrate from the USSR. In May 1980 she and her husband Vasily helped form an unofficial Emigration Committee, which collected information on Soviet Pentecostalists persecuted for trying to leave the country, and sent it to the United Nations and other international organisations. In May 1982 Vasily Barats was arrested for 'anti-Soviet agitation and propaganda' and given five years' imprisonment. Galina Barats-Kokhan was arrested in March 1983 while visiting him in Rostov prison. She was sentenced to six years' imprisonment and three years' internal exile and is due for release in 1992.

Lydia Lasmane-Doronina, a 60-year-old Baptist from the Latvian republic, is serving five years' imprisonment and three years' internal exile. She was arrested in January 1983 and convicted of sending information abroad about Latvian political prisoners. This is Doronina's third imprisonment on political grounds. In the 1940s she received a ten-year sentence for her part in nursing Latvian partisans, who resisted Latvia's unification with the

Soviet Union between 1945 and 1948. In 1970 she was sentenced to three more years' imprisonment for circulating a Latvian translation of a work by Aleksandr Solzhenitsyn. A widow, Lydia Doronina worked as a seamstress before her latest arrest and reportedly required regular medical treatment for tuberculosis, and for heart and liver complaints.

In 1977 **Olha Heiko Matusevich** became a Ukrainian Helsinki monitor, one of an unofficial group that documented allegations of human rights abuse in the Ukrainian republic. Although she left the group in 1979 she was arrested in Kiev the following year and given three years' imprisonment for 'circulating anti-Soviet slander'. On the day she was due for release in 1983, Matusevich was asked to sign a statement renouncing her former activity. She refused, was charged with 'anti-Soviet agitation and propaganda' and sentenced to a further three years' imprisonment. Now 32 years old, Olha Matusevich was formerly a teacher of Czech language and literature. Her husband, a fellow Ukrainian Helsinki monitor, is completing 12 years' imprisonment and exile, also on a charge of 'anti-Soviet agitation and propaganda'.

Before her arrest in March 1983 **Lagle Parek** worked as an architect in the Estonian city of Tartu. During the 1970s she appealed for the release of many Soviet prisoners of conscience, including Tatyana Velikanova, mentioned below. In 1982 Parek and 12 other Estonians wrote an open letter to 'the

citizens of the Republic of Finland', expressing fears that a new port built in Estonia by Finnish labour would damage local culture. Lagle Parek was sentenced to six years' imprisonment in an ordinary regime corrective labour colony and three years' internal exile. An appeal court, however, changed her sentence to imprisonment on *strict* regime. Parek, who is married, is now 44. She is due for release in 1992.

Natalya Lazareva, a former theatre director aged 38, was arrested in Leningrad in March 1982 and sentenced to four years' imprisonment and two years' internal exile for allegedly compiling an unofficial collection of feminist poetry and prose entitled *Maria*, and sending it abroad. This is her second imprisonment for political reasons. In 1980 she was sentenced to ten months for allegedly producing another *samizdat* almanac entitled *Women and Russia*. Lazareva is unmarried and has no relatives. Other inmates of ZhKh 385/3-4 report that she has suffered repeated punishments and that her health has deteriorated. She is said to suffer from cardiac insufficiency, ovaritis and a kidney complaint. Natalya Lazareva is due to be released in 1988.

Raisa Rudenko, a technician from the Ukraine, was arrested in Kiev in 1981 and sentenced to five years' imprisonment and five years' internal exile. She was convicted of smuggling poems from her husband's corrective labour colony and sending them abroad. Her husband, the writer Mykola Rudenko, is currently serving 12 years' imprison-

ment and internal exile as a prisoner of conscience for founding the Ukrainian Helsinki monitoring group. Raisa Rudenko is now 46 years old and said to suffer from a stomach ulcer, cholecystitis, nephritis and a heart complaint. For ten years before her arrest doctors placed her on a strictly controlled diet with limitation on meat, fish and salt intake. The diet in Zone 4 is reported to be totally inappropriate to her state of health.

[PUBLISHER'S NOTE: *Since these biographical notes were compiled by Amnesty, a further report has appeared in America. This states that Raisa Rudenko has disappeared: 'Nobody knows her whereabouts. This is possible under the Soviet penitentiary system.'*]

Now 31 years old, **Irina Ratushinskaya** is currently one of the youngest inmates of Zone 4. She is serving the maximum sentence for 'anti-Soviet agitation and propaganda' – seven years' imprisonment and five years' internal exile – and is not due for release before 1994. Irina Ratushinskaya is a physicist and poet, whose verse has been published abroad both in Russian and in English, French and German translations. She was arrested in Kiev in 1982 and convicted of contributing articles to an unofficial workers' bulletin, and of writing poems critical of the USSR. During her imprisonment Irina Ratushinskaya has been repeatedly punished for protesting about the treatment given to her and her fellow prisoners, and her health is said to have deteriorated. She reportedly suffers from pains in her kidney region, swellings and a chronic fever.

Sofya Belyak, also aged 31, is a Roman Catholic church organist from the Ukraine who was arrested in 1983 after officials had searched her home in Zhitomir. At her trial she was convicted of forming links with members of the unofficial Polish labour union Solidarity, and also of circulating leaflets about the miracle at Fatima, at which the Virgin Mary is said to have appeared to three Portuguese children in 1917. Belyak was sentenced to five years' imprisonment and five years' internal exile and is due for release in 1993. She is reported to have taken part in at least one hunger-strike in ZhKh 385/3-4 to protest against conditions of imprisonment. However she reached the zone only in the summer of 1984 and her name does not appear in the diary compiled until March of that year.

At the time this paper was drafted, two prisoners of conscience were due to have left Zone 4 to begin the second part of their sentence in internal exile. Both women played an active part in the events described in the *samizdat* diary. **Tatyana Velikanova** left the zone in 1983 and is now in internal exile in Soviet Central Asia. A mathematician, Velikanova has been an outspoken advocate of human rights since the early 1970s. She was arrested in 1979 and convicted of editing *A Chronicle of Current Events,* the oldest *samizdat* publication on human rights in the USSR. Velikanova was sentenced to four years' imprisonment and five years' internal exile. Now 53 years old she suffers from hypertension, angina, arthritis and ischaemia.

Tatyana Osipova, a computer programmer aged 36, was arrested in 1980 for her part in the unofficial Moscow Helsinki monitoring group. She served five years' imprisonment and in May 1985 was due to begin five years of internal exile. Instead, however, Amnesty International learned that Osipova had been faced with a fresh charge of 'malicious disobedience to the demands of the administration' and sentenced to a further two years' imprisonment under Article 188-3 of the RSFSR Criminal Code. It is not yet known where she will serve her new sentence. Amnesty International is re-adopting her as a prisoner of conscience since she is imprisoned for her non-violent protests against violations of prisoners' rights. Tatyana Osipova reportedly suffers from kidney disease, chronic hepatitis and endometriosis. Her husband, fellow Helsinki monitor Ivan Kovalyov (pictured with her), is also serving ten years as a prisoner of conscience.

UPDATE: This paper was prepared by Amnesty International's Research Department in June 1985. In July the Research Department learned that the inmates of the Small Zone had been transferred to another section of Mordovian corrective labour colony No. 3. Amnesty International is distributing this paper on conditions in the Small Zone since it describes the treatment the inmates received until recently and indicates the kind of conditions they may be subjected to at present. [July 1985]

Extracts from

THE DIARY OF
THE SMALL ZONE

Some of the Small Zone's 'internal regime regulations'.

AUGUST 1983

A full-scale campaign designed to break the morale of the prisoners in the Small Zone began in August 1983. We see a link between this and the circumstance that between April and August the quartet of resident prisoners was joined by by **Irina Ratushinskaya**, Jadvyga Bieliauskiene, Tatyana Vladimirova, Galina Barats and Edita Abrutiene. Evidently, the people who decide how we should be treated have got the idea that this is an appropriate time to tighten the screws and achieve the desired results by instilling fear of reprisals. There are indications of an attempt to poison our mutual relations to put us more on a par with the criminal prisoners. The Andropov era appears to be making itself felt. A convenient formal excuse for reprisals is our refusal to wear breast badges. This was not required before January 1982, and when the regulation was introduced it was applied in a half-hearted proforma fashion. In August the camp administration announced that they would take any action necessary to force us to wear them. We knew that breast badges alone give no protection against reprisals. (Lazareva's initial agreement to wear the badge did not prevent section chief Podust from barring her from the camp store, cancelling visiting rights and putting her in solitary on other pretexts.) But our KGB caretakers are very eager to force us, by threats and compulsion, to back down from our principles and succumb to their humiliating demands. Podust informed all of us about the decision to intensify the measures taken against us, saying, among other things, that none of us would be permitted to receive visitors or to enter the store for the rest of our terms unless we put on the insignia. We have explained our position on the insignia to the camp administration repeatedly, but they said they were acting on higher orders. For this reason we addressed an appeal to the Presidium of the Supreme Soviet. The wearing of breast badges is not the only humiliating demand made on us since the summer of 1983.

We were ordered to stand up whenever Podust entered the room, to call her 'citizen superintendent', to wear boots (the only officially sanctioned form of footwear) with our calico dresses when we went out in summer (slippers are permitted only indoors), not to leave our sewing machines during working hours (even though we always completed the norm anyway), always to wear kerchiefs (which were, in fact, never issued – 'we could have got them if we had really wanted to' –), and so on. Since August the guards have turned in a series of reports about our behaviour: for wearing 'non-regulation issue' skirts; for sitting at the sewing machines in our free time; for not wearing a kerchief; for lying in bed during the day (**Ratushinskaya** with a temperature of 38.8°C), and so forth. These reports were often concoctions written by someone else. The guards themselves were frequently unaware of what was written in their name. On the basis of these reports administrative orders (*postanovleniya*) were issued which included mention of the failure to wear breast badges. The absence of insignia was represented as a one-time offence (so-and-so many prisoners did not have them) and not as a general refusal to wear them.

At the same time they stopped giving us the texts of camp orders to copy, so that we could not quote and contest them. These actions were accompanied by threats: 'You're allowed only two sets of underwear. We'll do a search and confiscate the rest.' (Podust); 'It's high time you were put on a really strict regime, but you drink from enamel mugs and have cooking pans and an electric stove. It's time they were impounded.' (Assistant Colony Director Shishokin); 'How are you going to have children after a spell in solitary?' (Gorkushov, Chief of Operations, Directorate ZhKh 385/3); and so on.

Our vegetable plot received special attention. We were not entitled to it but we had always had one because the camp administration could not provide the regulation ration: 200 grams of vegetables and 400 grams of potatoes a day. Besides, the vegetable plot is the only source of vitamins here; they never give us greens. For those who cannot eat salted dripping or marrow (Rudenko is allergic to meat and meat stews, and we all have kidney trouble), this is the only source of nutrition. We cannot get permission to cook for ourselves, and, regardless of the fact that, for health reasons, most of us need a diet, they serve boiled and salted food. They blackmailed us with this vegetable plot a long time ago, but in July they proposed a 'compromise': if we put on the insignia, they would 'turn a blind eye' to the plot. On 13 August they dug everything up under the supervision of Podust. When she saw that the guards and the detail of criminal prisoners were reluctant to uproot everything, she flew into a rage and began pulling up the plants herself, including the ornamental peppers, which she tore from their tubs. We do not know where the uprooted vegetables were taken. The infirmary once served a soup made with beetroot tops, and that was that. They didn't even leave us the coriander plants and other aromatic herbs. At that time they were serving us pickled gherkins and gherkin soup.

On 9 August we were all given the order depriving us of the right to use the camp store for not wearing our insignia. **Ratushinskaya** also received the order cancelling her visiting rights for the same reason. This was because **Ratushinskaya**'s relatives wrote a letter incautiously announcing that they 'would come on 8-10 August'. The imposition of two concurrent punishments for one and the same offence was clearly illegal, so the zone inmates (with the exception of Vladimirova) went on strike. Three days later **Ratushinskaya**'s visiting rights were restored. On 11 August they told the oldest prisoner, Bieliauskiene (born in 1929), in the presence of her visiting relatives that she would be put in solitary if she refused to wear her insignia and that this would finally ruin her health. (Bieliauskiene was scarred with tuberculosis, had had her gall bladder removed and was suffering from kidney and liver infections.) Bieliauskiene replied that she would rather die than act against her conscience, to which Podust said: 'You'll be forced to anyway!'

On 17 August Lazareva and Osipova were taken into solitary confinement [SHIZO] for refusing to wear their insignia and for absenting themselves from work: Osipova got 10 days, Lazareva 13. At the time when she was absent from work Osipova was in fact washing dishes in the kitchen after breakfast, but the entry in the charge sheet read: 'Was observed in the dormitory engaged in private business.' (The workroom, the kitchen and the dormitory are all in the same building.) The others – Velikanova, Barats, Abrutiene, **Ratushinskaya**, Bieliauskiene and Rudenko – declared a strike (as we always did when someone was in solitary). Since Lazareva was sick (she had an inflamed appendix and a bowel infection; they didn't give her a diagnosis, but the treatment was the same as for dysentery), we also declared a hunger strike, with the exception of Bieliauskiene, whom we would not allow to join us because of her state of health. Osipova shouted all this to **Ratushinskaya**'s husband, who happened to be at the station, as she was being escorted to the boxcar. For this both Osipova and Lazareva were again deprived of their visiting rights.

On the fifth day of our hunger strike, when we were all very weak, Vladimirova (she never participates in our activities) began to threaten us with physical reprisals. Since then we have periodically heard that 'they'll turn (us) into a pile of corpses' and have received individual murder threats. All this has been happening with Podust's knowledge and in her presence.

On the seventh day of the hunger strike Velikanova, Rudenko and **Ratushinskaya** were 'isolated' in the infirmary. On the eighth day they were fed by force. Velikanova and **Ratushinskaya** resisted and were handcuffed and force-fed by six men. In the course of this procedure they banged **Ratushinskaya**'s head against the trestle-bed and poured liquid down her throat while she was unconscious. Velikanova revived her in the cell in the psychiatric section where they were locked up after the force-feeding. This windowless cell is never aired, and they were not taken out for exercise. They spent five days and nights under these conditions. Judging by the after effects of the feeding procedure (enlarged pupils, nausea, vertigo, and a headache which persisted for many days), **Ratushinskaya** was suffering from concussion, but the doctor did not examine her, although therapist Vera Aleksandrovna Volkova took part in the force-feeding and must have seen what happened. This story became the talk of the infirmary, and it was decided to stop force-feeding Velikanova and **Ratushinskaya**.

Lazareva was released from solitary confinement a day early, on 29 August. When she returned to the zone we called off the hunger strike, warning the administration that we would repeat our action if they put any other sick prisoner in solitary confinement again.

But after the hunger strike there was virtually nothing for us to eat anyway: they had destroyed our vegetable plot, they did not issue the vegetable ration, and they brought us oversalted food that was unsuitable for people who were ending a fast. A *zek* is entitled to 25 grams of salt a day, and, like it or lump it, they mix it into the food they serve us. While we were fasting they brought us white bread, butter, sugar, eggs, and so forth. When we ended our hunger strike this all vanished, of course, and they started bringing underbaked sour black bread. We picked out the pieces of congealed salt and fibres. Those who ate it suffered from nausea, stomach and kidney pains, and edemas. We felt worse than we did during our hunger strike. And, since we had lost our shopping rights, we could not buy food in the camp store.

SEPTEMBER 1983

They took Velikanova away on 5 September. We ask to let us know where she is now and if she is in good health. We know that she intended to hold her next hunger strike on 7-14 September 1983.

On 7 September we sent a statement to the participants of the Madrid Conference via the camp administration and (with the exception of Vladimirova) all declared an eight-day hunger strike in defence of our fellow citizens. This time there was no attempt to isolate or feed us. When we began our fast a KGB man from Moscow arrived in the company of some of the local brass but, when he saw that we intended to go through with it, he made no attempt to communicate with us. He just sniffed and left. On 14 September the Directorate's Chief of Operations, Gorkushov, put in an appearance. He asked us what our grudge was and assured us that we would not achieve anything anyway. He told us that we would be treated in accordance with 'higher orders' and that the regulations did not permit us to undertake actions on behalf of others, including our fellow citizens. That day a doctor examined us for the first time.

When we ended our hunger strike they took us to the camp store, where we were not permitted to buy food, and showed us a scene of unprecedented abundance – vegetables, fruit, pastries and jam. They did this although we were only entitled to purchase the basic necessities (it is illegal to take away this right). But they refused to sell us even those, saying that we must first write a request for permission to make the purchases, which the camp director would then grant or deny. Since it was illegal to deny us the basic necessities we had no intention of writing such a request, despite Gorkushov's assertion that it was quite in order to take such measures against us. Instead, we wrote complaints to the prosecutor's office.

On 20 September a commission from the Main Directorate of Corrective Labour Institutions (GUITU) arrived (hence the abundance of wares in the camp store). That day they served us unsalted buckwheat porridge and butter (although, for the third day in a row, they forgot the bread) and showed us off to the commission at table. After the commission's arrival they sold us the basic necessities, started serving less salty food, and made an effort to issue the vegetable ration. The administrative orders (we were denied purchasing rights in the camp store in September and October, too) referred only to our refusal to wear insignia without adding any trumped-up charges. Since then Podust has put in only two appearances and has behaved quietly. On the whole they have been feeding us quite well since the second hunger strike. During the first few days they even served unsalted soups without bones, so even Rudenko could eat them. The publicity, our refusal to make concessions and the fact that 'they didn't know what to do with us' (thus camp director Pavlov) probably played a role.

When we ended our second hunger strike on 14 September we were freed from work for three days, after which they demanded that we fulfil the norm, indicating that if the full norm (70 pairs of gloves a day) were not met, there would be reprisals. We couldn't produce the norm, of course. We were all afflicted with edemas, some of us were running a temperature, and others kept on fainting, but the doctor was on leave, and the nurse could not or did not want to do anything. On 19 September four of the zone inmates were clearly in need of urgent medical attention. We called for a doctor from six in the morning to two at night on 20 September, but the duty physician who finally came said that he could not arrange hospitalisation for everyone in the middle of the night and that it was not his job to release them from work. He agreed to examine only those who were in a really bad state. The next day a woman doctor came and examined everyone but did not say anything about releasing us from work or reducing the norm for a few days. Only after a week did we learn whose medical certificates had been extended and whose not. When Vera Alexandrovna Volkova, the physician assigned to our zone, returned from leave, we learned that the Operations Department had banned the acceptance of medicines mailed to us in special packages. Now medicines and medicinal herbs have to be sent in regular packages – two a year – and in parcels, if they are not confiscated. She also confirmed that the classification as a third-degree invalid which the VTEK Examining Commission granted Lazareva in February 1983 had been annulled in May 1983, when she was in the infirmary after isolation, without Lazareva's knowledge or an appearance before a medical board. She is now required to meet the full work norm, of which she is physically incapable. We do not know what Lazareva's diagnosis was. When she was examined, nothing was established except a chronic inflammation of the appendix. They even contrived 'not to observe' the clearly visible effects of a spinal injury, her almost permanently high temperature, her vertigo, and her cardiac pains. From June to August Lazareva was treated for dysentery, but they did not give her a diagnosis and refused to perform any analyses before she was put into solitary confinement. Volkova, however, signed the solitary confinement order. The prosecutor's office answered our appeal by saying that 'there were no contra-indications against Lazareva's internment in a solitary confinement block'. Now that we have no greens or raw vegetables Lazareva has developed dermatitis because of the lack of vitamins.

We keep insisting that Lazareva be hospitalised and examined, and her reduced work norm be restored, but expect a possible repetition of the old story. We intend to declare a hunger strike if the sickest inmates (Lazareva and Bieliauskiene) are put in solitary again, because we believe that this would endanger not only their health but also their lives. If any of the others gets solitary, the rest will declare a regular strike.

OCTOBER 1983

Bieliauskiene was hospitalised on 20 October. The physician who treated her, V.F. Gun'kin, said he was not aware that Bieliauskiene's gall bladder had been removed and that the operation scar was no proof. 'Who knows, maybe they just opened you up.' He refused to put her on a diet.

On 25 October Bieliauskiene was visited by representatives of the Directorate's Political Department, Senior Lieutenant G.P. Votrin and Captain A.N. Uchakin, who were accompanied by Podust. They came in connection with Bieliauskiene's request to the Main Directorate of Corrective Labour Institutions that, in the event of her death, her body be sent to her next-of-kin. She was convinced that she would not survive her term under the existing conditions. Votrin told her that the standard procedure in such cases is for the Special Section to inform the relatives of the deceased immediately. He said that they are entitled to claim the body but must go to the Directorate to fill out the documents. Bieliauskiene explained why she had made the request, saying that, after her operation, the physician had instructed her to follow a strict diet if she wanted to live and that she was forbidden to eat almost everything they serve in the camp. Podust, who kept on breaking into the conversation, said: 'We have a lot of that kind of sick people here. If you're given a diet, they'll all demand the same.'

On 25 October we learned from a letter that Abrutiene's husband and nine-year-old son had come to visit her on 14 October, but the camp administration had told them that, prior to their arrival, Abrutiene had been deprived of her entitlement to two visits – one long and one short. Abrutiene knew nothing of this. She had received only one notice depriving her of visiting rights for refusing to wear a badge.

Furthermore, according to Article 53 of the RSFSR Corrective Labour Code, a prisoner can be denied only the next scheduled visit, not the next and the one after next.

NOVEMBER 1983

On 25 October Abrutiene submitted a written request for the restoration of her entitlement to one of the visits. There was no reply.

On 15 November we summoned Camp Director Pavlov and demanded an explanation. He threatened to punish us for coming out in each other's defence and said that the denial of two visits was legal. However, as it transpired, he did not even know why this action had been taken. Abrutiene, Barats, Bieliauskiene, Lazareva, Osipova, **Ratushinskaya** and Rudenko declared that they would go on strike until Abrutiene's visiting rights had been restored.

On 14 November Lazareva and Vladimirova were ordered to report for relocation, without being told the destination. Lazareva was ill, and they had promised that she would be sent to hospital for an examination, but they dragged their feet, claiming that there was 'no room'. On 14 November she had a temperature of 37.3°C and complained of stomach pains; she had had cardiac pains for the whole preceding week. Even though they measured her temperature twice, Senior Lieutenant Podust and Assistant Colony Director Shishokin maintained that Lazareva was simulating. However, they did not take her away for relocation that day.

They came for her again on 16 November. She was still sick and bedridden. She summoned the doctor. Assistant Colony Director Shalin said: 'Get ready, the doctor will examine you in the guard room, and if you have a temperature, we won't take you anywhere, of course.' We demanded that her temperature be measured in our presence. Dr V.A. Volkova took it; it was 37.3°. She left without a word, after which Deputy Regime Superintendent Major Pazezin, appeared, with Colonel Shlepanov, and several warrant officers and women from the hospital service. Shalin announced that Volkova had reported her opinion: Lazareva was fit for transportation. He said that, if she did not come of her own accord, she would be dragged away by force. Osipova and **Ratushinskaya** took up a protective stand in front of Lazareva's bed. They twisted their arms and pulled them away from the bed. They dragged Lazareva, who was barefoot and almost naked (she was wearing only panties and a blouse) out of her bed and into the frost. Shlepanov told us that Lazareva was being sent 'for re-education' to a KGB isolation prison in Saransk. Since Lazareva screamed and called for help, they beat her up on the way. She lost consciousness but remembers how Assistant Colony Director Shalin kicked her with his boots. In Saransk they refused to protocol her injuries; a whole week passed before a doctor examined her and made a note of the remaining bruises and scratches. Lazareva refused to talk to the KGB officials about anything concerning her own case or about her friends. She filed a complaint to the court about her beating, but we do not know if the case will be accepted and heard.

Abrutiene, Barats, Bieliauskiene, Osipova and **Ratushinskaya** lodged a protest, demanding that the prosecutor's office institute criminal proceedings. Osipova and **Ratushinskaya** declared that they considered it their duty to alert public opinion in the Soviet Union and abroad to Lazareva's fate. In addition, Osipova and **Ratushinskaya** demanded that the Medical Board of Directorate ZhKh 385 examine and treat Lazareva.

On 16 November **Ratushinskaya** and Rudenko were told that they were to be hospitalised. They made themselves ready. The guard Kiseleva checked their things and ordered them to leave their letters behind. Until now no one had ever prevented us from keeping letters (as we are entitled to do by law). We know that if you leave letters in the zone they can be confiscated or stolen (last year when they took us all to Saransk, a lot of things (including letters) which we left behind after the administation assured us they would be safe simply disappeared). Rudenko left her letters behind, but **Ratushinskaya**, invoking the *Rules and Regulations*, insisted on her right to take hers with her (she was aware that the KGB were displaying a lively interest in her correspondence; a physician (?!) had questioned her pregnant Kievan friend Liliana Varvak about it in the maternity home). The head of the Regulations Section, Lieutenant Suraykin, said that in this case the letters must be screened: 'Who knows what kind of notes you may have written on them?' **Ratushinskaya** suggested that they be checked on the spot, in her presence. Suraykin said he would send someone from the Operations Section. They took Rudenko to the infirmary but left **Ratushinskaya** behind.

Nobody from the Operations Section ever appeared. Starting on 18 November, **Ratushinskaya**'s condition deteriorated; her temperature went up, and her kidney pains became more severe. When Dr Volkova was summoned she said that **Ratushinskaya** had been registered for hospitalisation since 16 November but had, allegedly, refused to go. She added that if she were really ill she would agree to anything to get treatment. **Ratushinskaya** stated that, on the contrary, she insisted on receiving treatment but could go to the infirmary only under escort and nobody had been ordered to take her. Volkova replied that if she did not make any concessions she would not be hospitalised until the end of her term. Nevertheless, even though she did not give in and kept her letters, **Ratushinskaya** was hospitalised on 24 November. We do not know what is wrong with **Ratushinskaya**; she was in perfect health when she was imprisoned. She first requested medical assistance in April 1983, but so far they have neither treated her nor given her a diagnosis.

On 30 November before the examinations had been completed,

they unexpectedly summoned her to receive an injection. They refused to say what they were going to inject and did not state their diagnosis. **Ratushinskaya** said that she would not let them inject her with an unknown substance and demanded that they tell her what it was. Doctor Gun'kin said: 'That's none of your business, and if you protest I'll sign a release form.' The next day she was summoned for an injection again. This time they told her that they were only going to inject vitamins. **Ratushinskaya** did not object to this, and the injection was made.

DECEMBER 1983

On 2 December **Ratushinskaya** was unexpectedly discharged from the infirmary 'for violation of the regulations for in-patients and refusal of treatment', as they put it. She returned to the zone with the same temperature she had when she was hospitalised and demanded that this be protocolled. She had had a high temperature throughout her stay in the infirmary (37.5° on average), which was measured twice a day. In addition, she caught a cold while she was hospitalised and again developed acute edemas. On 7 December she summoned Dr Volkova to examine her. Volkova sent her for a chest X-ray. The same morning she examined Osipova (Osipova's chronic pyelonephritis was in an acute phase, her analytic values were bad, and she had pains and a high temperature). On 7 December Volkova prescribed a course of treatment with 5-NOK. Half an hour later **Ratushinskaya** and Osipova were put in solitary confinement for striking: **Ratushinskaya** for 12 and Osipova for 15 days. On 19 December Lazareva got 14 days solitary 'for resistance'. Since Lazareva was seriously ill Osipova, Matusevich and **Ratushinskaya** declared a hunger strike until she was released. The others, who were continuing their regular strike for the restoration of Abrutiene's visiting rights, had an additional reason for refusing to work and wrote statements declaring their moral support for the hunger-strikers. Osipova returned from solitary confinement with a temperature of 37.5°, which rose to 38.3° by the evening. Her lungs were crepitating, the state of her liver and kidneys had deteriorated, and she had a cough. **Ratushinskaya** returned with worsening pains in the kidney region and edemas. The same day she requested medical assistance and is still waiting for it. The average air temperature in the solitary confinement cell (we smuggled a thermometer in) was +13°, the maximum +15°.

On 23 December **Ratushinskaya** got 12 days in solitary 'for failing to appear for work without a plausible excuse' on 19, 20, 21 and 22 December. On 19 December **Ratushinskaya** had just returned from her previous spell in solitary and immediately summoned the doctor. She showed V.A. Volkova her serious edemas and told her that the pain in the region of her right kidney had become stronger. She demanded immediate medical assistance. **Ratushinskaya**'s day temperature was normal, and the doctor refused to give her medical aid and left. In the evening **Ratushinskaya**'s temperature rose, but she was not examined then or on the next day.

On 21 December **Ratushinskaya** went on hunger strike to demand that they release Lazareva from solitary and give her medical assistance. Despite **Ratushinskaya**'s illness after solitary confinement and the hunger strike, the administration declared her fit for work. Volkova signed their report, claiming that a doctor is not permitted to release someone from work during a strike.

The fasting **Ratushinskaya** was put in the same punishment cell as Lazareva. In the solitary confinement block Lazareva was being fed as usual. The cell was cold, but they did not succeed in measuring the temperature this time. Lazareva's condition kept on deteriorating. She wrote to the Medical Board, asking them to improve the conditions of confinement in view of her illness and to give her medical assistance, saying that, otherwise, she would declare a hunger strike on 26 December. She was examined by a doctor who diagnosed cardiac insufficiency and ordered a urinalysis. Lazareva did not receive medical help and began her hunger strike on 26 December. For the duration of the hunger strike neither Lazareva nor **Ratushinskaya** was given a bed, although they demanded one, the sleeping boards were locked up during the day, and they had to lie on the floor.

During the night of 27-28 December Lazareva had two heart attacks; she was wheezing and gasping for breath. On both occasions **Ratushinskaya** called for a doctor immediately, but no one came. On the evening of 28 December a nurse, without entering the cell, told them through the serving hatch that Lazareva's urinalysis was 'excellent' and that, therefore, the doctor would not come. From then until 2 January Lazareva lay on the floor next to the radiator (which was almost always cold), and, although **Ratushinskaya** kept on asking for help, she received no assistance except from **Ratushinskaya**. Lazareva had two more heart attacks, her appendicitis worsened (she was writhing in pain), and she experienced nausea and vomiting.

JANUARY 1984

On 2 January, when she was due for release from the punishment block, Lazareva could not stand up and had to be carried. **Ratushinskaya** declared that she would not end her hunger strike until she had seen for herself that Lazareva had reached the zone alive and had been hospitalised.

Ratushinskaya left the solitary confinement block on the 15th day of her hunger strike, 4 January. She broke her fast after she saw Lazareva through a window in the infirmary. Dr Volkova examined **Ratushinskaya** (blood pressure 100/60, temperature 37.3°C) and said that, in view of her temperature, she would release her from work for that day and would take another look at her the day after (by this time she had found out that she was entitled to release hunger-strikers from work). On the following days **Ratushinskaya**'s temperature persisted, rising to 38°C in the evenings.

Abrutiene, Barats, Bieliauskiene, Matusevich and Osipova have appealed to the prosecutor's office over **Ratushinskaya**'s term in the solitary confinment block.

Osipova indicated that, as a protest against the inhumane treatment of **Ratushinskaya**, she would continue the hunger strike declared in connection with Lazareva's solitary confinement until **Ratushinskaya** returned from the punishment block.

On 24 December (the fourth day of her hunger strike) Matusevich broke her fast for health reasons following Podust's statement that the temperature in Lazareva and **Ratushinskaya**'s punishment cell was 18°C.

On 29 December Bieliauskiene began a hunger strike in protest at Lazareva and **Ratushinskaya**'s punishment.

On 4 January after **Ratushinskaya** returned from the punishment block and Lazareva's hospitalisation, Bieliauskiene, Osipova and **Ratushinskaya** ended their hunger strike.

This time no one was fed by force.

On 5 January the Deputy Head of the Section for Political Education, Shalin, Podust and Arapov (a section chief in the men's zone) came into our zone and invited Osipova to have a talk. They suggested that she end her strike. Osipova replied that she would resume work as soon as Abrutiene was allowed to have a visitor. Shalin informed Osipova that Article 188-3, which made it possible to impose an additional five-year term on prisoners who maliciously violated regulations, had been introduced into the Criminal Code. Osipova said: 'The administration has a strange logic: you will break the law, but we cannot protest because the Code includes this Article 188!' Podust, who kept on breaking into the conversation, summed up with: 'It would be a great pity, Osipova, if you were to be released in 1990 instead of 1985.'

Shalin said that Abrutiene and **Ratushinskaya** had been punished correctly because prisoners are obliged to work while on hunger strike, also if in the isolation cell.

On 20 and 21 January Lieutenant Colonel Pavel Polikarpovich Artem'yev of the Mordovian Directorate of the KGB summoned all of the inmates of the Small Zone (with the exception of Lazareva, who was in the infirmary). He announced that he had been appointed to replace Belov as head of the KGB Directorate at ZhKh 385. Barats, Bieliauskiene, Osipova and **Ratushinskaya** refused to talk to him. Doronina said she could talk to him only about religion and the rest made a number of demands of the administration. Artem'yev insisted that they talk to him about something and said to **Ratushinskaya**: 'You don't want to talk to me but you're going to have to anyway, because circumstances can arise in which you can't turn to anyone else except me, and then you will ask me for something and I shall be silent. Would that be a good thing? I don't have anything of the sort in mind, but don't you, for example, have beds in which you grow "flowers". Well, you'll have to turn to me in the summer.'

On 26 January Ganichev, the prosecutor at ZhKh 385, visited the zone (for the first time in several years). With **Ratushinskaya** he conducted the following dialogue:

RATUSHINSKAYA: Why won't they give me (a copy of) my sentence?

GANICHEV: Was the trial open or in camera?

RATUSHINSKAYA: Can a trial under Article 70 be held in camera?

GANICHEV: Yes, it can, if state or military secrets or compromising details about someone's private life are revealed.

RATUSHINSKAYA: Nothing of the sort was revealed at my trial, and it was open.

OSIPOVA: Besides, a sentence is always public anyway.

GANICHEV: Yes.

RATUSHINSKAYA: Then why won't they give it to me?

GANICHEV: Since they won't release it they must have the right.

RATUSHINSKAYA: On what grounds?

GANICHEV: There are normative acts regulating the treatment of people in your category. They are secret, and I will not show them to you.

RATUSHINSKAYA: Who issued them?

GANICHEV: I won't say.

RATUSHINSKAYA: But what if they contradict the law?

GANICHEV: They don't. In the ordinary zones, where there are thousands of people, everybody has a copy of his sentence. They have long since smoked them or flushed them down the toilet. But you lot here know all the legal codes, so you are covered by normative acts.

RATUSHINSKAYA: Does that mean that there are secret laws in the USSR?

GANICHEV: There are military regulations and other instructions, not everyone is entitled to know them.

RATUSHINSKAYA: So there are secret laws?

GANICHEV: That's what it means.

RATUSHINSKAYA: But why is it so dangerous for me to know my sentence?

GANICHEV: If there is concern that it might be used for anti-Soviet purposes (*we* do not know whom you are going to read it to or to whom you might give a copy), the number of people who are allowed to see it is restricted.

To our question as to whether we are obliged to work during a hunger strike Ganichev replied that, according to the instructions concerning hunger strikes, prisoners must fulfil all legal 'demands of the administration'. 'If you are on a hunger strike you still must fulfil the work norm 100 per cent, march in formation and not advertise the fact that you are fasting.'

On 30 January Osipova and **Ratushinskaya** were sent to the punishment block for failing to report for work and refusing to wear their breast badges. Osipova told Pavlov that he had no right to put her in solitary because, since that morning, she had had a temperature of 37° (measured in the presence of Volkova) and it would undoubtedly rise further. Podust, who was also present, interjected: 'That's a normal temperature.' Pavlov hesitated and then signed the punishment order: 13 days. **Ratushinskaya** got 15 days. Osipova and **Ratushinskaya** sent statements on the conditions of their detention in the punishment block to the Office of the Prosecutor of the Mordovian ASSR. The two statements were identical.

While she was in her punishment cell **Ratushinskaya** complained to the doctor about her edemas and kidney pains. Treatment was prescribed, but she refused to accept injections or tablets until she was told what they were treating her for and what with. They told her the names of the drugs at once but tried to avoid giving her a diagnosis; however they finally gave her two: pyelitis and chronic pyelocystitis. While they were in the punishment block Osipova and

Ratushinskaya felt that they were running a temperature but were unable to obtain a thermometer: the nurses said that there were only two thermometers in the sick bay and that too many prisoners were already ill with flu.

FEBRUARY 1984

On 7 February, Ganichev's deputy, Osipov, came to the camp. On February he visited Osipova and **Ratushinskaya** in the punishment block. **Ratushinskaya** began talking about Abrutiene's visiting rights. Osipov said that he had told Abrutiene the day before that she had been deprived of her visiting rights legally. **Ratushinskaya** asked him: 'On what grounds do they demand that we work during a hunger strike?' Osipov said: 'That cannot be. Take yourself, for example, they didn't force you, did they?' **Ratushinskaya** replied that they had indeed forced her and put her in the punishment block for not working while she was on a hunger strike. 'What?!' Osipov exclaimed. 'We'll check on that.' But the next minute he started saying that prisoners are obliged to work during a hunger strike too. In reply to Osipova's question as to which day a hunger striker must be examined by a doctor and what the work norm should be, Osipov replied: 'You have to fulfil the norm 100 per cent, and nobody is obliged to examine you as long as you can walk. You'll be examined as soon as you keel over.'

On 8 February Edita Abrutiene and Jadvyga Bieliauskiene were put in the punishment block, Abrutiene for 15 days, and Bieliauskiene for 10. As soon as she arrived at the punishment block Abrutiene wrote a statement demanding that Artem'yev be summoned. Two hours later a KGB official called Tyurin arrived. The gist of the conversation was that Abrutiene explained that it was not to the KGB's advantage to put us in solitary or treat us badly, because we are the mirror of their humanism and it would only harm the Soviet regime if we were to leave the labour camp as sick women. Tyurin asserted that the administration, not the KGB, had been putting us in the punishment block. They had a similar conversation on the next day too.

On 8 February Abrutiene, Osipova and **Ratushinskaya** wrote a protest to the prosecutor's office about Bieliauskiene's internment in the punishment block and sent an appeal to Directorate chief Khamlyuk in which they offered to serve Abrutiene's present and all future spells of solitary confinement for her.

On 9 February Osipova and **Ratushinskaya** made the same suggestion to Tyurin, explaining that they were making an exception to their refusal to talk to the KGB because the punishment block could cost Bieliauskiene her life. For this reason they were appealing to anyone who could help to obtain her release. On their return from the punishment block they declared hunger strikes (from 12 and 13 February respectively) until Bieliauskiene's release. After Bieliauskiene's return on 17 February Matusevich, Osipova and **Ratushinskaya** ended their hunger strike.

MARCH 1984

On 26 December Rudenko was transferred from the infirmary to Kiev. The trip from Moscow to Kiev was made by plane. In Kiev she was confined to the KGB investigation block. Neither in Mordovia nor Kiev was she informed of the nature, purpose or justification of the transfer order. For the most part she was interrogated by the KGB officials Gonchar and Il'kiv from the Operations Department, at the end of her stay in Kiev by the head of the Operations Department.

They kept on talking to Rudenko about **Ratushinskaya** and Matusevich: 'Is **Ratushinskaya** playing cock of the roost nowadays? Why is she so vicious?' 'What does Matusevich talk about?' Rudenko said that, in the zone, she mostly talked about their work. She was granted a one-hour meeting with her brother and, on the next day, with her mother. They asked her if she would like to go to the theatre or on an excursion. She refused. They told her that she could join her husband in exile if she would promise not to engage in anti-Soviet activities. Among such activities they included conflicts with the camp administration. Rudenko gave her word of honour that she wouldn't. They asked her to give it in writing. She refused and repeated several times that she would not engage in anti-Soviet activities any more. They explained that if she were to give her word in writing they would present the paper in the event of her breaking it. Besides, they said, the KGB could send a pardon appeal to the Supreme Soviet. Rudenko also refused to write a petition requesting a pardon. She returned to the zone on 2 March.

In a letter from her husband **Ratushinskaya** learned that in January the camp administration had answered his telegram enquiry about her state of health by saying that she was well. **Ratushinskaya** has been running an almost constant high temperature for several months now (usually $37.3°C \pm 0.2°$) and suffers from persistent edemas and kidney pains. Her condition had been the same in January. **Ratushinskaya** wrote Pavlov a statement asking him to reply truthfully to enquiries about her health. Two registered letters in which she described her state of health in detail 'got lost' in the post.

We suspect that, besides 'losing' letters, the authorities may also be forging them. Accordingly, we ask you to pay close attention to the texts and the handwriting.

Artem'yev came on 7 March. He entered our building, saying that he wanted to congratulate us and have a chat. He regretted that he had not brought any flowers. Then, for some reason or other, he left and sent a guard to escort us to him one at a time. Abrutiene spoke with him in the same vein as with Tyurin. He gave her chocolate, which she brought back into the zone. He had two talks with Rudenko: one in the zone, when, as she put it, he spoke about nothing in particular; the second in his office, when he asked her why she refused to give a written commitment not to engage in anti-Soviet activities. She replied that if they didn't trust an oral promise they wouldn't trust a written one either.

Doronina and Matusevich also went for talks. Artem'yev complained that the others did not want to talk to him. He offered Matusevich chocolate too (which she refused) and explained that he had brought chocolate for each of us but wanted to present it to us personally. Nevertheless, he did not offer chocolate to Rudenko and Doronina. **Ratushinskaya** refused flatly to go for a talk, saying that such talks were not prescribed by law and were not part of her obligations as a prisoner. If it were really necessary (she said) they would have to send an armed escort and use force. Artem'yev told her through a guard that she was violating the regulations and that he was entitled to penalise her. They didn't send an escort, and **Ratushinskaya** stayed put. Artem'yev did not summon the rest of us.

We remind you that there is no women's punishment block at camp ZhKh 385/3 and that they send us to the block at Corrective Labour Camp No. 2 (settlement Yavas), where cell no. 7 is reserved for us.

The guards in the punishment block had been ordered to confiscate Lazareva's and Osipova's warm clothing. This time they were not permitted to keep their own slippers or warm undervests. Lazareva and Osipova refused to wear the slippers that were handed out to them because the regulation-issue footwear is old and dirty and is not disinfected, and a lot of people in the punishment block get fungal infections. **Ratushinskaya** got one during her last spell of solitary. They were sent to the cell in their stockinged feet.

The next day, 15 March, the chief of the Regulations Section, Ryzhova, called them to the duty room to check whether the guards had done their job conscientiously and taken away all of their non-regulation clothes. When she saw that they were wearing woollen sweatshirts she ordered their immediate confiscation and promised to punish the guards who had overlooked them. She also ordered the confiscation of their kerchiefs, which all women in the punishment block are entitled to wear in winter and which all of the criminals there were wearing. Lazareva was also ordered to take off her stockings. She refused to undress, and they threatened to handcuff her and undress her by force. At this Lazareva removed all her clothes and set off for the cell naked. The guards chased her down the corridor and persuaded her to put her clothes on. They gave her stockings back to her. On 17 March their kerchiefs were returned and they were allowed to wear their own slippers. We were told unofficially that the order to confiscate their clothes came from the KGB.

On 14 March **Ratushinskaya,** who had been in the infirmary since 12 March, declared a hunger strike for the duration of Lazareva's solitary confinement. They tried to persuade her to give it up and offered to make an entry in her medical record to the effect that a hunger strike would endanger her life. **Ratushinskaya** refused. They released her from the infirmary on 15 March.

On 16 March Abrutiene and **Ratushinskaya** were ordered to get ready to transfer to the punishment block. **Ratushinskaya** called for a doctor. A nurse came. It was established that **Ratushinskaya** had a temperature of 37.9°. Then three physicians came and measured her temperature with two thermometers. This time it was 38°. They demanded that **Ratushinskaya** either end her hunger strike or sign a statement that she refused a medical examination. She refused to do either. Abrutiene was sent to the punishment block alone, for 15 days. **Ratushinskaya** was isolated for eight days in a cubicle in the psychiatric division.

On 26 March *kurator* Viktor Nikolayevich Yershov, the KGB overseer of our zone, visited Abrutiene. He gave her food, treated her to tea with lemon, and sent her back to the cell with a cucumber and some shortbread biscuits. They had a long talk. Yershov was especially interested in **Ratushinskaya** and asked if she really ate nothing when she was on a hunger strike. Abrutiene replied that **Ratushinskaya** really does fast.

In the middle of April Vladimirova was called to the camp director. A KGB official was present in his office. She said they asked her 'how Osipova and **Ratushinskaya** push up their temperatures' (both have been feverish for a long time, **Ratushinskaya** almost constantly). Vladimirova said that solitary confinement 'helped'. They asked Vladimirova to write a statement saying that Abrutiene had been 'dragged' into the strike and claimed that they already had one statement to this effect. Apparently, from the viewpoint of the KGB, the situation in the zone is not sufficiently conflict-laden and they have decided to plant a false report.

In April the letter situation took a big turn for the worse. At this time **Ratushinskaya**'s correspondence almost ceased. The letters she wrote were either confiscated or lost. The same thing happened to letters sent to her. At the beginning of the month the censor said that letters have to be collected and delivered by the section chief. Everyone, including those who talk to Podust, declared that they would neither accept letters from or give letters to Podust. Only Matusevich agreed to do this. Now, as before, the censor is our letter carrier. In the middle of April the censor said that she would no longer explain which parts of the text of a letter had led to its confiscation. She had been forbidden to do this and said that we ourselves know what we are not allowed to write. At the same time letters were confiscated from Lazareva, Osipova and **Ratushinskaya**. From **Ratushinskaya** they took three postcards with the text: 'Congratulations on International Labour Solidarity Day. I express my solidarity.'

At the end of April our unit chief, S.E. Gainichenko, was transferred to other work. Section chief L.N. Podust has been transferred to Tambov. In April she was promoted to the rank of captain. She is winding up her work here, waiting for her children to finish the school year. The administration avers insistently that Podust's transfer is in no way connected with our demand for her removal. Deputy Political Officer Shalin is now performing the duties of unit chief and will, apparently, be confirmed in this position.

APPEAL

We, women political prisoners, wish to speak of our fellow-prisoner **Irina Ratushinskaya**. Her fate deserves the special attention of the people of the world; her fate depends directly on this attention.

Irina Ratushinskaya is the youngest woman prisoner in the Mordovian concentration camp.

Irina Ratushinskaya is the first woman to receive the maximum term under Article 70, part 1 (anti-Soviet agitation) – seven years' labour camp plus five years' exile.

Irina is a talented poet whose poems have flown to every corner of the country like swallows of freedom, a woman of clear and incisive intellect, a courageous and active defender of human rights. Intellect, talent and fearlessness – the KGB considered this combination especially dangerous.

She is being persecuted in the camp too: by the denial of her right to buy food in the camp store and of her right to receive visitors, and by confinement under conditions of torture in the punishment block for refusing to wear a mark of humiliation (a breast badge), for continuing her struggle for human rights, dignity and liberty, and for setting an example to others in this struggle.

She has not even been given (a copy of) her own sentence – an unprecedented violation of the law.

We are permitted to write only two letters a month, but this is evidently considered too much for **Ratushinskaya**: her letters are regularly confiscated or mysteriously 'lost' en route, and the same thing happens to letters sent to her, so that no word comes out of or into the camp.

Irina, who came to prison a healthy woman, has been sick for many months now. She is tortured by kidney pains, edemas, and a constant debilitating fever.

Despite her illness she has repeatedly declared strikes and hunger strikes in defence of others, thus attracting new reprisals against her.

But they have not succeeded in breaking her. She has kept her cheerful temperament and readiness to come to your help at any moment. Here is an example.

In December, fresh out of the punishment block and sick herself, **Irina** immediately declared a strike in support of the sick Natalya Lazareva, who had been put in solitary. Although she was fasting and running a temperature they put her back in the punishment block. In this icy stone tract she saw in her new camp year. On New Year's night **Irina** supported Lazareva, who lay ennervated, and declaimed poems to the criminal prisoners in the neighbouring cells.

Irina has over five years of camp before her, and if they are like the first she will simply not survive until the end of her term. We appeal to all people of good will to speak out in defence of Irina Ratushinskaya so that she may be spared the tragic fate which normally awaits Russian poets.

Galina Barats, Jadvyga Bieliauskiene, Lydia Doronina, Natalya Lazareva, Tatyana Osipova, Lagle Parek.

[1984]

NO, I'M NOT AFRAID

My Motherland

Now, what if I don't have any right to put that as a title? Is it possible for a person not to have a motherland? Or do I have one in spite of everything? But then what should I consider my Motherland to be?

The nationality column in my passport says I'm Russian. Well then, is the answer Russia? But I didn't visit geographical Russia until I was quite grown up, and even then I only saw the fringes of it – Moscow, Leningrad – that was all! And what did I get out of it? Did anything stir in me at the sight of those much-sung birch trees? I must admit it didn't. And anyway, birch trees for some reason don't grow in Odessa. Well, all right: I was born in Odessa. On the map Odessa's in the Ukraine. So: Ukrainian culture, the Ukrainian language, and Ukrainian customs; the Ukraine: *it* is my motherland, of course.

But just a moment: ask anyone who's ever been in that town – don't let them tell you lies, now! – what sort of Ukraine Odessa represents. Don't misunderstand me – I can understand Ukrainian, I can write it and read books in it; but speak it? I lived in Odessa for 24 years, but never once did I have to do that. There's no one to speak it with, the language doesn't have any bearers. The Odessa dialect, though it's based on Russian, is none the less in a category of its own. So many languages, turns of phrase and even special intonations are mixed up in it that it's a sort of Tower of Babel, a multinational.

But, as the Secretary of the Odessa Komsomol Committee said when he banned the annual show 'Humorina' – a specifically Odessan celebration –: 'Odessa has great revolutionary and working-class traditions. There can be no question of there being any other kind of specifically Odessan phenomena.'

And so 'Humorina' was banned, and transferred to Tver', where, of course, it didn't catch on and luckily faded away. As was evidently the intention. Let's never forget that we, the generation who were born in the full flourishing of Soviet power, and who in order to be educated were given into the hands of specialists trained in advance by the Soviet authorities, must get one thing into our heads: our Motherland (with a capital letter) is the entire Soviet Union, from one frontier to the other, and the immense Siberian *taiga* is every bit as much our motherland as the Baltic States, for example. We're the masters of both those places! And if we decide to chop off a bit of Finland, or Poland, or Japan in the same way – then they will also be our Motherland, the same one which we have to love until the tears come, and for which we have to be ready to lay down our lives. There is, of course, no normal person who could ever have such a conception of motherland.

So what else is left? Poland? Yes, my great-grandfather met his death during the Polish uprising; yes, then my antecedents had their estates confiscated and moved to Odessa. But I learned Polish from books, and read Polish literature, or that part of it which was allowed by the Soviet censorship; it was from the works of the stormy petrel Maxim Gorky that I got my earliest conception of the Polish national character, as a stream of the most impudent bad language, put for politeness's sake into the mouth of a gypsy woman (a simple, politically illiterate woman, not the author himself).

Because – I shouldn't ever forget it – the Soviet regime had already managed to kill any interest my parents – the descendants of gentry – had in their origins and antecedents. There were, after all, one or two other people who were interested in our origins!

'We shall let it all go, the past, we shall forget our bloodlines – they're not without risk, after all – we're Soviets! And only Soviets.' And so in my family the Polish language – 'no, you mustn't!' – fell into disuse. And then how many times was my grandmother, a practising Catholic, hauled in by the KGB because she visited the Polish Roman Catholic Church! But here too my parents protected me: not only did they forbid grandfather and grandmother to teach me Polish; they also forbade them to talk to me about any religious or "un-Soviet" subjects. Otherwise they wouldn't allow me to have a professional training! And thus the last threads which connected me to my family's past were broken.

What was left to me in its place? Soviet education? Literature? Certainly! My mother herself taught literature in a school, didn't know the difference between Pasternak and Balmont, and knew Blok only as the author of 'The Twelve', and that was the way I was to learn, too! It was only later that I found out about the Silver Age of Russian literature; at that time the only thing I was supposed to know was that, unlike Mayakovsky, the decadents were mediocre writers whose only aim was to distract the Russian people from the revolutionary struggle. Culture? As much as you like!

Let the reader try the following mental experiment. I say 'mental' because, once again, no normal person could ever bring himself to do such a thing – yet this was done by a whole people!

Take a book you haven't read and, using a blunt saw, shred off a portion of it – a quarter, say. Now, from this portion attempt to understand the contents – but first destroy the remainder, so you won't be tempted to look. That was what was done to world culture for us – 'the new generation of Soviet mankind'. I should hope so, too! After all, we were being earmarked for life under communism!

And so, living in families whose members all had Soviet higher education, in a school with a prescribed system of education, in a network of libraries with carefully selected literary texts, special television programmes, books and journals – how could we hope to obtain knowledge of any other reality? Indeed, we didn't even know of the existence of that 'other reality'! And a kind of electric shock leapt through me when I was 24 and in the space of a single week read, almost simultaneously (I was only able to borrow the books for a short space of time), Mandelstam, Tsvetayeva and Pasternak! They literally knocked me off my feet, physically: I was in bed with a fever and delirium. The abyss opened up before me – but, unlike in other nightmares I had had, I wasn't on the edge of the abyss – oh no! I was down at the bottom of it, inside it, and the edge was somewhere unattainably far above me! All my ideas about Russian literature and history began to crack and give way. And all this was on top of the attacks of rebelliousness I was always subject to. Was it my Polish genes playing up? I don't know. But for some reason I was never able to accept the Soviet religion, although I knew no other. What kind of God-seeking can one do if one doesn't even know one's motherland? And I didn't do any seeking. God himself found me, and helped me to endure, and nurtured my soul, because there was no one else to nurture my soul during my childhood and youth.

I estimate that my Soviet education set back my development by ten years. It was at 24, not 14, that I acquired an understanding of genuine culture and genuine history. It was at 25, and not 15, that I began to write. Yes, I had, of course, made earlier attempts, but they were merely the scrawlings of a child who – through no fault of her own – knew only half the alphabet. At the moment I'm 27. Yes – one bout of eager gobbling is enough; after that, one can make up for lost time and, perhaps, bridge the gap.

Some day – if I live that long! – I'll make up those years. What is there one can be certain of in this fine world? If I live. If they don't put me in jail. If they don't send me to a mental hospital. Do I stand much of a chance? That's a rhetorical question, dear reader.

And it's one I don't have the answer to.

[1982]

As the flags roam about Red Square,
The rabble of birds bawls in its wheeling above the ramparts. . .
They have made us swear the oath by means of deception.
But it isn't true — I haven't sworn any oath.

1. FROM THE BULLET TO THE ROPE

Not for me twenty years on

Not for me twenty years on
To forget the freedom of my youth,
Incline my grey head guiltily –
And close the springtime window.

Not for me the fate of one day meeting
My friends with their strained voices,
Hearing the judgement passed on them – and being silent,
Following them helplessly with my eyes,
And feeling the imprint of betrayal.

Let the majority control the laws –
It has been granted a different season.
But I don't know whom I have to thank
For the right to my first escape.

[Odessa, September 1978]

And I undid the old shawl

And I undid the old shawl –
And at once there came to me
The four winds from all the roads,
From the clouds of the earth.

   And the first wind sang me a song
   About a house behind a black mountain,
   And the second wind told me
   About an enchanted arquebus.

And the third wind began to dance,
And the fourth gave me a ring.
But the fifth wind came laughing –
And I recognised his face.

   And I asked: 'Where have you come from?
   And who has sent you to me?'
   But he looked into my features
   And said nothing.

And I touched his shoulder –
And sent all the others away.
And this wind blew out the candle,
When night fell.

[Kiev, November 1978]

Passer-by

Passer-by, don't drink the water in this town –
Its salt with the taste of summer
Will make you fall mortally in love!
Don't lay your head down – the years will stop.
You have not completed the Path –
Remember that.
Don't forget your goal in kind houses,
Don't surrender the dusty
Happiness of pavements . . .
Do you hear how quiet it is? But the angels have flown away.
Let your heart be accomplished outside their power.
Don't kiss a female hand in the human thicket:
Be afraid to remember April –
The smell of gloves!
Let your forehead be imprinted with the sign of the Path,
Let your lips be proud,
Passer-by!
Do not love.

[Odessa, 1979]

No, don't save, don't preserve

No, don't save, don't preserve,
We've grown so unused to protection!
O, we're not at all those poets
Who seek armour in verses –
We are not serfs and not a retinue.
In our pride – go on, punish us! –
Not bending our knee . . .
Don't admit us to the final paradise,
Only save from corruption
What to us – alone – is law and honour,
That we may grow by our breathing
And say our verses out loud
Though we dare not say our names.

[Kiev, 1980]

And here I go flying down the steps

And here I go flying down the steps –
Almost in somersaults – as in a dream.
And the day is springlike to the point of madness,
And the yard with its streets is – springlike!
And there is no salvation
From the storming devil in me.
    Oh, how urgently I need to go
    There where it's bluer than blue –
    To splash in the puddles by the faucet
    To frighten the pigeons away from the eaves!
How rapidly they change places –
Step, bound, leap –
The cold resonance of the doorway
And the sudden burn of the sky!
    And there's a smell of tomcats and hops
    From the dried flagstones.
    And I pant with April
    And shout to my brother – 'You look miserable!'

[Kiev, 1980]

One should not ask for help

One should not ask for help.
This world has been created
                      in masterly fashion
Why try to guess what will happen?
The bitterness has already passed.
I shall go to be reflected at midnight
In the empty mirrors
                      of barber shops
And be extinguished many times over
On the other side of the glass.

On the border of the water
                      and the moon
I will not delay for a moment –
I will stride, my head thrown back,
I will slip the palm of my hand
                      into the emptiness.
And I will become a chance reflection,
A fleeting optical illusion –
Like the reflection of the girl
Who is not
        on the bridge.

Oh, what a spring it's been!

Oh, what a spring it's been!
All April – under the sign of the station.
The spring, how criminally it trembled –
Spoonbait thrown aslant!

Smashing the wooden pointswitch
Open – by means of the moon –
It passed over insomniac pavements
And doubled my shadow behind me.

How it stifled me in its arms – the rogue,
How it cared for me, saying – don't die!
Neither Russia, nor blizzards, nor Pestel –
Here it is, your promised land!

Do you recognise them – leaf with its bitter taste,
Pale circle of old music,
Salty laughter and light of straw?
Hands that are cursed can't be disjoined!

How the reed-pipe came in floodtides,
How the ebbtides vexed us – never mind –
How happy we were
At two weeks' remove from 'forever'!

How bravely we read the story
With its ending about sweet smoke . . .
It has left, that springtime train.
It has left alive, thank God!

I shall write

I shall write about all the sad people
Who have remained on the shore.
About those who have been condemned to silence –
I shall write.
Then burn what I have written.
Oh, how these lines will soar,
How the sheets of paper will fall back
Under the fierce blast
Of irreparable emptiness!
With what haughty movement
The fire will outstrip me!
And the ashen foam will tremble.
But give birth to nothing.

But we shall remain

But we shall remain
On the squares of the monstrous chessboard –
We are all convicts.
Our coffee
Smells of burnt letters,
And a smell of opened mail fills
The post offices.
The high-rise blocks have gone deaf –
And there's no one there to shout 'Don't!'
And the stucco faces on the house fronts
Have closed their eyes.
And every night
The birds fly out of the town,
And blindly
Our dawns are lit.
Wait!
Perhaps this is only a dream.
But in the morning
The newspapers appear.

The Ballad of the Wall

May we receive, then, in the highest measure!
We sang together –
We are placed apart,
Momentary knights
Of orders that pierce the breast through!
It's quick.
Already in the gunsight
Are the white mouth and the eyebrows' division.
May we receive!
And there is no bed
More vertical or more white.
From nightmares of a nocturnal scream
You emerge and intercept me,
Oh my devotion to a face
Which has not finished singing
To the heavens!
And on the burnt-out masonry
Against which the shoulder-blades must press to their uttermost
From two last steps away I see –
The imprint
Of two wings.

There is a far-off planet

There is a far-off planet.
The water there is green.
Above the water the cities
Have been forgotten somewhere by someone.

The columns are covered in tiny cracks,
The warm stone is like a living being,
Braided with the half-drowsy
And impudently growing grass.

Between the white houses
Silence tautly slumbers.
The engraved characters have been washed
From the slender towers by the long rains.

But the planet has forgotten everything,
Everything has grown over with grass.
The wind whispers: there was something,
Something was, and passed.

And the springtime sings with its breezes,
The water slowly weeps.
And a fabled star
Stands above the cities.

Wisely and anxiously
The fish peer out of the river,
Through the dark grasses the beetles
Are timidly making their way.

The birds are happy in their flight,
The white light is eternally radiant . . .
Perhaps one day there will again be something
After many, many years.

Two versts from the river Dvina

(To my great grandfather –
Lieutenant Colonel of the Civil War)

Two versts from the River Dvina,
With a bullet in your throat –
In your last agonies –
In the middle of your war
You threw back your arms forever.

And over your white shirt – the blood
Is blue.
And your mouth is bitten through.
And the simple souls
Of bewildered ants
Dance in a round dance.

Instead of future summer days,
Instead of bitter posthumous glory –
In the overrun depths
The grasses
Wail above you.

Your thunderstorm
Has drifted off.
We are sunk in the shame of alien parades.
But your eyes have been given me –
As a curse
And as an award.

Why

Why
Do half our escapes take place in dreams?
(Oh, don't worry – they won't catch up with us!)
The darkness has dried up. Only to survive!
But on the morrow –
The other half.

From the living, who direct fate with cold fingers,
Out of the trap of the mirrors,
Which the avid folds covered
As though they were oysters – run!
Don't feel sorry about what's there behind you,
Behind you there is nothing.
There they're already tearing at the leash!

Across the desert of the asphalt,
Across the dry land –
Leaving
A trail that never grows cold,
Losing our way
Unable to ask for protection –
We leave, run, pant . . .
Before us
No Moses.

Our letters will burn to ash

Our letters will burn to ash – and it will be a good September.
The migrations of the birds will die away – and our losses will flow over.
A bitter-sweet calm
Will be poured over our hearts
By the light above the cherry tree, and the house on top of the hill –
And everything will be as we wished it.

We'll heal all our wounds,
We'll forget as soon as we hide our eyes.
We'll all get together and drink some lively wines.
And with smiles we'll remember the tale of the prodigal son –
The émigré who went back to plead guilty.

Don't ask yourself: 'Am I a poet?'

Don't ask yourself: 'Am I a poet?'
They won't take long to make you one of their poets.
All the means – from the bullet to the rope –
Are freely available to you.

And when your human flesh begins to wander
You'll understand, remembering this motif:
'From Yelabuga* to the Black River,
My motherland is wide.'

[Kiev, 1981]

* *Yelabuga was the remote Tartar town in which*
Marina Tsvetayeva hanged herself.

Leningrad Triptych

I

No one will raise this city's eyelids.
Only don't try to run – the streets have been dug up.
In the city of the dead the living must answer.
Can you hear their boots on the cage of the staircase?
    In this oblivion the grass won't grow for an age,
    In this silence one can only shout in one's sleep!
    Our breathing is the trophy of the local winter
    And the snow doesn't melt on the lips of the passers-by.

II

And so,
Watering of a Black steed
Beside the Black River.*
A splash of twill!
And the officers have risen beside the water.
And so – the snow above the white plains,
And the taste of freedom melts on our lips.
Our move is from cage to cage.
No, don't cry.
Accept that it's not for you – the crown of a queen.
Don't cry, don't dream.
My square formation is deadly.
How simple to wound my planet in its flight:
Not by a stroke of the pen – by a single movement of the hand . . .

Don't do it.
Don't look over there.

It's not the first time there's been such a December
Above the white plains –
A mixture of wings and bullets
Why should we know
Why the river is flowing black?

* *The Black River flows through the outskirts of Leningrad.*

III
(to N.L.)

Mother of God, why is it dark?
Wouldn't you like me to light
The green icon-lamp?
Or perhaps we'd better not.
Like a little girl, you look out of the window:
Whose footsteps are these in Petrograd?
It's still a question that affects you.

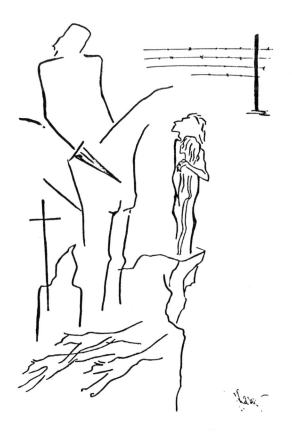

How unfortunate for the parade

How unfortunate for the parade:
On the Palace Square – it's raining!
The shields on the façades are streaming,
The proletarian leader is floating
In something sticky,
The flags are getting wet,
And criminal wetmarks are spreading –
Over the placards, the rags, the paper –
Like the diamond-red steam on the executioner's block.
The silhouettes are already eyeless,
But will serve to frighten the children.
Crashing in unison on the wet stone
The parade passes over the Square.
But the Square is ill and compliant,
Its eyes are tight shut – not a window!
Its perimeters are surrounded
By a red rabble and black blood.
They'd close in – enough of words –
Turn brutal, break loose from their places . . .
But they don't dare – so stubbornly
Does the stern angel bear the cross aloft!

2. AFTER THE FIRST ARREST
(December 1981 — September 1982)

The Sparrows of Butyrki

Now even the snow has grown sad –
Let your overwhelmed reason go,
And let's smoke our cigarettes through the air-vent,
Let's at least set the smoke free.
A sparrow flies up –
And looks at us with a searching eye:
'Share your crust with me!'
And in honourable fashion you share it with him.
The sparrows know
Whom to ask for bread.
Even though there's a double grille on the windows –
And only a crumb can get through.
What do they care
Whether you're on trial or not?
If you've fed them, you're OK.
The real trial lies ahead.
You can't entice a sparrow –
Kindness and talents are no use.
He won't tap
At the city double-glazing.
In order to understand birds
You have to be a convict.
And if you share your bread –
It means your time is done.

[11-20 December 1981]

Where are you, my prince?

Where are you, my prince?
On what plank bed?
(No, I won't cry: I promised, after all!)
My eyes are drier than a fire.
This is only the beginning.
How are you coping?
(No, I know:
Better than all the others. Oh, to take your hand!)
Winter's draughty curtain
Drives the winds round in a circle
To the point of despair,
The air was too exhausted
To leave its rags on the grille.
Are you falling asleep?
It's late.
I'll dream of you tonight.

[18 December 1981]

Wearing an idiotic jacket

Wearing an idiotic jacket –
It used to be a child's overcoat –
My head full of rhyming rubbish,
I was as happy in Odessa as no one:
I had neither half a kingdom, nor a horse, nor a bridle!
    In Odessa I was like a cicada in someone's hand:
    With neither oaths, nor tears, and salt measurable in *puds*.
    Fly away, return – the dusty honey-grass
    Will take away my pain, and the blue sky and mussels in
        the saucepan.
My streets have been worn through to holes,
My staircases have been licked away by helter-skelter running.
My rocks are gleaming like backs from the water,
And my cathedral has been swept away from Cathedral Square.
    But when I grow tired,
    The cathedral will rise up again where it was –
    I shall take a ticket back there, one way –
    To the lanes, the warm evening, memory and dust!
    And my gypsy woman will sell me a sweet.

[21 January 1982]

How ineptly fate goes around

How ineptly fate goes round
Collecting her quit-rent!
Twenty-five years without you –
That is the first term.
Ten days apart from you –
That is the second term.
Well, what's the third,
Which isn't far distant?
It's no longer than the first, after all,
And no hungrier than the second . . .
Open the door to the poor woman –
And laugh sinfully at her.

[1 February 1982]

Mermaids, and stars with rays

Mermaids, and stars with rays,
And waterlilies in carved letters –
What sadness was implied
By the vignettes in those battered books!

In what confusion they said:
'Oh, we understand . . . go on, grow!
But remember: anyone over six
Won't see the most delicate plants.

Don't be afraid, they won't wither,
The wild beasts, too, will remain here,
And the letters will last forever
And they will steal your heart away.

You will grow attached to other toys,
But you will love us beyond the threshold of blindness . . .
Look: here are parsley leaves,
And here are angels, and flowers!'

[7 March 1982]

On Batyev Hill

On Batyev Hill –
There our house stood.
As on black silver –
In white silver.
    A three-week habitation,
    A temporary shelter.
    The wine we have not drunk
    Others will drink.
There was nothing to lose –
And the keys were in one's hand:
Inhaling January,
To draw breath.
    Three concrete walls,
    A strip of glass . . .
    Three weeks of silence,
    Light and warmth.
All the locks had been tamed,
We brought bread . . .
On the table the written sheets
Piled up like snow.
    But then we had to say goodbye –
    Grief was no trouble!
    It was no longer hard
    For us to live – anywhere.

[1 April 1982]

Oh, I see you

. . . .

O, I see you – however hard you close your eyes –
You stand inextinguishable.
Above my homeland – my first or second? –
*Szara godzina** is falling.

I shall not drift through the streets, through the patrols
Like the wind of nocturnal Gdansk.
Like a wounded dog my heart aches in silence –
If only I knew the right word!

If only I knew the Polish word –
It cannot be otherwise –
That grants freedom!
With what's left of my breathing to forget all my songs
For a lofty ode!

So that everything goes into your bonfire,
Your church, your surf –
The colour of ash and chalk . . .
The blood on the intersections, like the train, rumbles with you:
Nie zginęła!†

---

* *Szara godzina*: 'the grey hour' – twilight (Polish).
†*Nie zginęła*: 'I'm still alive' (Polish).
The beginning of this poem is missing.

It seemed to you that it was night

It seemed to you that it was night, a searchlight at the window.
Waking, you leapt up.
But it was only the dawn.
The hour before the alarm – hour for last dreams, my kindred one.

The hard day lies ahead. But that the birds –
Not yet in the foliage –
In the swelling branches, along the first down –
Are squalling,
That means today the woods will explode in green.
Try to go back to sleep.
Release over their accustomed route –

$\qquad\qquad\qquad\qquad\qquad$ your sails and flight.
How many minutes are left there?
They won't get them,
No one will get your sails.

[16 April 1982]

I had a strange dream

I had a strange dream last night:
I was to be shot at dawn.
I was imprisoned in a concrete basement
From which the dawn was not visible.
And then one of my classmates appeared,
We were sitting together at the same desk,
Copying out exercises from each other
And throwing a paper dart
(For some reason it wouldn't fly).
My classmate said: 'Good evening.
How unlucky you've been. I'm very sorry.
I mean, being shot – it's so inhumane.
I've always believed in soft measures.
But somehow no one asked me,
They just gave me a pistol and sent me.
I'm not here alone, you know, my family's here,
I've got a wife and kids – a son and daughter.
Look, I can show you their photographs.
My daughter's like me, don't you think?
You see, I've got an old mother.
I mustn't put her health at risk.
The council gave us a new flat just recently,
It's got a pink-tiled bathroom.
And my wife wants a washing machine.
I mean, I can't . . . Anyway, it's no good . . .
There's nothing we can do to change things.
I've a pass to go to the Crimea, to a sanatorium.
I mean it'll all be the same to you . . . at dawn.
If they hadn't sent me, it'd have been another.
Perhaps somebody you didn't know.
And after all we did go to school together
And throw paper darts together.
You've just no idea how bad
It makes me feel, but what can you do?'

I had a dream
(Dedicated to my friend Valery Senderov)

I had a dream: steeds and horse-cloths,
A hand with a prickly ring on my shoulder,
And the bitter face of a brown icon,
And the solid murmur of a thousand swords.
After that I don't remember. The grasses grew tired
Of lamenting injuries, the wolves of howling,
And someone sang over the corpses at the transit camp,
And our wounds dried up, and we were thirsty.
It was August. The stars grew ripe
And fell into the campfires of the soldiers,
And it was still not too late to save the Motherland,
So it seemed to us. We waited for the hour,
We rose – and in saving for the umpteenth time,
We walked into the grass and ceased to be.
A crazy girl ran barefoot
Among us with a cry. Not to kill –
It's so simple! Just when I think
My motherland is going to absorb the guileless lesson . . .
No! The waters rust, the women wail.
And we shall rise up when the moment comes.

[December 1982]

My hateful motherland

My hateful motherland!
There is nothing more shameful than your nights!
How lucky you were
With your holy fools,
Your serfs and executioners!
How good you were at spawning loyal subjects,
How zealously you destroyed
All those who could not be bought
                  or sold
But who were condemned to love you!
If your frightened ones are innocent,
Why are your nightingales silent?
Why on the profaned crucifixes
Do your tears
        freeze?
How I dream of your crucified ones!
How quickly in their footsteps I must follow
You –
    akin,
        accursed –
And go to a similar death!
By the most terrible road you possess –
The brink of hatred
           and love –
Dishonoured, wretched,
Mother-and-stepmother,
             bless me.

The incoherent radio

The incoherent radio crackles its short waves.
You can't hear a thing –
A sentence, but how many years? And on whom?
Between us there is only the fragile substance of a glass table –
And a bedraggled angel mopes in the cigarette smoke.

And who is he going to be able to protect –
This unconsidered fledgling –
Gauchely feathered,
With the dark eyes of another country,
Knowing other customs, ignorant of fear and weeping –
There's nothing to indicate whose this waif may be,
This Savoyard!

Onto whose shoulder will he fly –
Between the door and the chain?
With whom will he share his asphyxia
And in his silent turn
Exchange dole for ration –
Tatters for rags –
And the tracery darning of bars for a simple window-sash?
And why has he got himself mixed up in the nightmare,
Where the snow has no reply,
Where from birth to execution you choose but one of those two?
He doesn't know, he's asleep –
Shielding himself from the light with his palm . . .
He's used to interference.
No point in turning up the sound.

O Lord, what shall I say

O Lord, what shall I say that hasn't been said before?
Here I am under Your wind in my canvas clothes,
Between Your breathing and pitch-black death –
O my Lord!

What shall I say at Your interrogation, if I'm ordered
Not to be silent, but to turn and face my country –
With its deadly amusements, its rags of parting, deaf and dumb –
O my Lord!

How will You dare to judge,
According to what tribunal?
What will You answer, when I force my way through and arrive –
When I stand up and lean my shoulder against the glass partition –
And look in,
And ask You for nothing.

We're untranslatable

We're untranslatable in literal terms.
What are poems? The odour of cigarette smoke,
Not for the smoker but for those at his side.
An aroma that has ceased to be a poison.
Blue herbs. A matter of no weight.
And when there's a smell of burning,
That's how it's supposed to be.
Everyone knows it.
The banner remains untorn
Only until the first battle.
Higher! There, it's already in tatters . . . With you is
God,
And those who follow you cannot be harmed;
Only their hair smells of smoke.
There is no other fate.
It's a family trait of Russian poets
To be shot at, like banners.
And it's done by roster.

[1982]

Oh, I've forgotten how to tie a bundle!

Oh, I've forgotten how to tie a bundle!
But my grandmother knew how.
Is it so hard to wrap up our earthly goods
In a white scrap of cloth?
What shall we take with us?
The notebooks will get used up,
The bread will go hard.
All the same, let's perform the farewell ritual –
Let's tighten crosswise the handkerchief we've chosen,
Each as best he is able.
Pick it up – and may God go with us!
The grass won't bend under our feet,
So weightless are we.
We shan't turn round and we shan't reproach.
Why should we show our torment to him –
The unexalted?
Later he'll choke, somebody's captive,
In the damp warmth . . .
Is it worth lingering right on the city limits?
How stylised we are on this local canvas!
It doesn't even hurt.

Why let your eyelashes freeze

Why let your eyelashes freeze –
Our farewells won't take place today.
And we've more than one stretch to go on these roads –
But our émigrés' fate's meted out to us in advance:
That of the station foundling
Abandoned in a third-class carriage.

We take with us a curse –
For not having kissed the right hands.
This ill-intentioned earth will never be any kinder to us.
All the same, we'll return,
But with altered eyes,
To the mortal snow-love
Of her winged Decembers.

And then
Let her take account of my generation's pain,
The pride of its wanderings,
And its orphan's five-copeck bit –
In expiation of her motherly virtues –
Let it all be taken fully into account.
But then let her sins be pardoned.

Tell me the truth

'Tell me the truth, gypsy woman,
Why have I dreamt of the wind?'
'Falsehood. He loves you.
But to dream of the wind means a journey.'

'Tell me, gypsy woman, the truth –
Is our fate to be found in my palm?'
'Give me your hand. He loves you.
But this means a long journey.'

'Gypsy woman, tell me, why
Has our candle burnt down?'
'That means a parting soon
And the very longest journey.'

'Gypsy woman, tell me that this
Isn't true! Tell me, gypsy woman,
That is isn't *that* journey!'
'Don't be afraid. He loves you.'

My overseas Septembers

My overseas Septembers,
We shan't dream of each other any more.
City of low lamp standards
That get in behind one's eyelashes,
You, breeding your clowns
Where time is a speechless wall,
You, who are able to laugh like that
As other people break their bread –
I wish you – fair weather!
Smile. I shall hold my breath.
Look – I'm one of your kind.
I won't spoil our farewell with tears.

Our days have not been completed

Our days have not been completed,
Our souls have not been put to the test,
And when the birds fly away
We are not ashamed of our songs.
We wander through the crazy town
In our ugly modern clothes,
And our tiny sadnesses
Wring their dry little paws.
Harmless witnesses,
We're not worth a bullet in the back.
We are soundlessly leaving,
Having snuffed out the candles behind us.

How we love to guess what will happen
After our speechless departure!

Perhaps the nights will be different –
And no one will notice the wind.
The summers, perhaps, will be colder –
And our poets will be forgotten.
And our tears will have come to nothing,
And our faces will have been effaced.
And our lips will no more be remembered,
Lips that didn't know how to kiss!

Ineffectual modern children,
We are leaving – with a wish
That someone should burn our letters
Out of pity, without reading them.

With what care we snuff out the candles –
So as not to drip wax on the tablecloth!

From an unfamiliar window

From an unfamiliar window
A meagre light trembles and flows:
And the reflected moon
Floats like an apple in a well.
And that is all.
Not a dog and not a star.
The minutes drip – but miss . . .
Like one's heart the fruits sink earthward
But the tremor of the earth is imperceptible.
Who has ordained this hour for us –
This speechless prospect of the soul?
Shall we seek to justify ourselves?
Shall we accuse time, growing impassioned?
Shall we pine for far-off ones without tears?
And strain to hear their call, though neither their voices
Nor the sound of their fetters are audible.
But in the midst of silence
Is it possible to take this disfavoured call
For the absolution
Of guilt?

[16 September 1982, night]*

* Irina Ratushinskaya was arrested on 17 September 1982.

3. AFTER THE SECOND ARREST

(October 1982 – April 1983)

Steeply the stars are scattered

Steeply the stars are scattered, and cold in the settlements of the
        heavens.
This moon is on the wing – hold on, don't let your grip slacken!
It closes your eyes – and beyond the limits of tired vision
A skater, like a pair of compasses, draws measured circles.
In winter's black-and-white engraving nuances disappear,
The stern poverty of phrases rumbles like an oration.
Five paces to the window and four from wall to wall,
And the mounted eye blinks through the iron.
The monotonous guile of an interrogation trails past,
The young escort is guilelessly coarse in soldierly fashion . . .
Oh, what calmness – to wander silently through the winter,
Not even allowing the word 'no' to fall from cracked, sewn-up lips!
The snowy pendulum has worn away: how many weeks have passed?
Only the eye is darker above the poem, the forehead hotter.
Through heat and cold – I will reach, I will reach April!
I am already on the road. And God's hand is on my shoulder.

[October 1982]

Pencil Letter

I know it won't be received
And won't be sent. The page is in tiny shreds
No sooner than I've finished scribbling it.
Later. Some day. After all, you're used to it,
Reading between the lines that haven't reached you,
Understanding everything. And on the tiny sheet
I find room for the night, taking my time.
What's the point of hurrying, when the hour that's past
Is merely part of the same term, I don't know how long.
And a word stirs under my hand –
Like a starling. A rustle. The movement of eyelashes.
Everything's OK. But don't sleep yet.
A little later on I'll tie up my sadness in a bundle,
Throw back my head, and on my lips there'll be a seal,
A smile, my prince! Even from afar!
You'll feel my hand warm
Across your hair. Across the hollows in your cheeks.
How December has blown on your temples . . .
How thin you've grown . . . Let me dream of you more, more!
Open the window. My pillow is hot.
Footsteps behind the door, and a bell tolling in the tower:
Two, three . . . Remember, you and I never
Said goodbye! This is nothing.
Four. Everything. Such a heavy tolling.

[3 November 1982]

The path grows steeper

The path grows steeper – the time
I have been waiting for has come.
And there's not enough air for my windpipe,
But the pain of height is radiant.
The icy film crackles
As it freezes into the spring,
And the heart flies up into the steepness
Like a young black goat.
And further – through flint and brimstone,
My footsteps ever more weightless,
But here my soul is measured
In the highest degree.
And if I get there – above the land
I'll see the bridges of rays,
But if I don't – punish me with death,
My sky-blue honour!
Oh how many of us there are and have been
On this mountain path!
Only an echo – a swotting schoolboy –
Keeps saying:
                    'It's time! Fly!'

[November 1982]

It's the first of January

It's the first of January –
Yet we don't have to sweep out a single fir-needle!
And my neighbour grumbles all morning
Trying to sweep out her frustration.
And then suddenly gives a roar.
I don't go to her: what help can I give her?
'Exercise!'
The red carpet.
The drunken faces of the guards.
To get along the corridor as quickly as possible
(Through the chlorine, bits of food, urine, putty)
And out into the air! Into the concrete yard!
Sixty minutes are already ticking away.
The clink of keys. And the sound of good-natured laughter:
'A bit of exercise'll do you good, girls!'
And my neighbour: 'Oh, I wish you'd all . . .'
The rest's not fit for print.
Five paces from wall to wall.
Netting above us – you won't fly away!
And just before she woke up this morning my neighbour
Dreamed of John the Baptist.
She dreamt he'd been brought to her cell.
As if he'd been on the march – so tired.
He was covered in grime, and his feet were caked with dust.
And how sorry for him she was!
She tore off a piece of her towel
So he could wash his feet.
He took it. And said to her: 'It's hard
To be alive, but your time is done.'
And he got ready to fly. Then a radiance
Began, and she cried:
'Let me see my daughter!
You can do it, see if you can't!'
But he gave her no sign
Either with a hand, or with a wing. He was silent.
She even thought he might be weeping.
That means – there will be sadness.
Or maybe a misfortune?
In the morning the dream came true . . .

And she – so unlucky! –
Wanted just this once to dream of something happy!
'Now then, that's enough of your gymnastics'
(This to me) 'Come on, you can't go on jumping up and down
For the whole hour! And don't spend
So much time writing in your exercise book – get some sleep!
Why, whenever I look at you, 🌸 you
Staring? Do you like me – or hate me?
It's just that this is the third year I've spent in here.
But I wish you well . . .'
I nod. And again – start running.
How many months – running on the spot.
How many dreams I run to you,
Tying them up, as in the sticky dough,
In the smell of chlorine, in my sheet,
The torn rags of the dirty walls . . .
Is there any place from which one can love more powerfully
Than from here? Not on the cross – but
In the torment of the Judas holes,
In the sophisticated boorishness of the interrogators,
In the agony of my neighbour's dreams,
In the blue smoke of her cigarette,
In the fierce pity I feel for her – ill,
Brought halfway to death,
Hysterical, kind and angry,
And cursing whoever it is who spins
This globe – in the nonsense
Of days without sun and tears without makeup –
More intensely, more sacredly – nowhere
Is it possible to love, my love!

[December 1982]

The Spider-Mathematician

The spider-mathematician (hard to imagine a sorrier creature!)
Keeps trying to count his thin little legs.
But sensibly he doesn't believe the tiny number he ends up with
And angrily mutters: 'The damned thing won't work out again!'
He has woven diagrams, assiduously measured the angles,
He solves the problem of which is the wolf and which the goat
With a cabbage leaf, but doesn't believe the result and once again
Rustles hopelessly and sighs: 'I know the answer, but how to
        prove it?'
O potty genius, crucified on coordinates,
Eccentric Pythagoras, half-witted prison prophet!
Wait before you creep away: I believe your results!
Spread out your diagram, and count the days of my sentence, please.

[January 1983]

122

And it's turned out

And it's turned out to be simply boring –
No more than that. The cramped space
Of the cell, the enclosure in the stuffy courtroom –
A comfortable, oakwood barrier
Between me and the judges – so they won't get confused.
Eye to eye! A childish triumph!
They're coming back! Are they afraid of uproar in the court?
Does my cheerful gaze seem fierce,
Like a convict's? Do they dream I'll get them by the throat?
But my brigandage has already been overcome
By the pride my forefathers chiselled out:
What have these servile eyes to do with me?

[In the courtroom, 1 March 1983]

Some people's dreams pay all their bills

Some people's dreams pay all their bills,
While others' gild an empty shell . . .
But mine go whimpering about a velvet dress,
Cherry-red and sumptuous as sin.
O, inaccessible! Not of our world!
Nowhere to get you, or to put you on . . .
But how I want you!
Against all reason's reproaches –
There, in the very narrows of the heart's
Recesses – flourishes the poison
Of heavy folds, and obscure embroidery . . .
The childish, flouted right
To beauty! Not bread, not domicile –
But unbleached, royal lace,
Enspiralled rings, sly ribbons – but no!
My day is like a donkey, bridled, laden,
My night deserted, like the prison light.
But in my soul – it's no good! I am guilty! –
I keep on sewing it, and in my mind I make
The thousandth stitch, as I do up my anorak
And try on my tarpaulin boots.

[April 1983]

124

That traitress and apostate

That traitress and apostate,
That mote in the government's eye,
That especially dangerous criminal –
What a joke! – she's cutting a tooth.
It knocks like a chick in an egg, thrusts out,
Quite oblivious of everything.
So what if the window's covered in iron?
It goes on growing – and it's spring, too!
My sentence is awaiting confirmation,
The Supreme Court is in session . . .
I ought to be whimpering for leniency –
But my seditious tooth prevents me!
It stews its way out all morning,
Like a starling gobbling my head . . .
My good-for-nothing wisdom!
You've chosen a fine place to assert your rights!
What's to be done? Tomorrow there'll be a search!
They'll discover you, raise a hullaballoo,
And the guard will get a ticking-off
For not being watchful enough . . .
The regulations forbid the possession
Of this sharp, cutting object!
'What do you mean, it just grew? That's impossible!
There's nothing about it in the rules!
What foolish pranks is she up to, the impudent hussy?
Have you ever heard of the like?
Other people lose their teeth,
But she's gone and grown a new one!
What if it's something she got in a parcel?
Perhaps it's some crafty prosthetic appliance
Containing a TV camera? Paid for,
Of course, by the NTS!'*
And my papers will pass along the tables,
And the prison governor will sigh:
'Hurry up and pack her off to a camp!'
Be patient one day more!

---

* *NTS:* a right-wing émigré organisation.

My country has a humane Supreme Court
For recalcitrant poets:
They'll confirm my sentence, and off I'll go.
Perhaps this time I'll grow wings!

[April 1983]

4. POEMS FROM THE SMALL ZONE

(From April 1983)

Over the cornfields

Over the cornfields roamed the pre-war wind,
And an odd fifth-form boy, in love with everything in the world,
Using whole candles over MAGELLAN's maps,
Was meanwhile growing up. Everything was going
According to plan, wasn't it, Lord? Under the cold sky
He hallucinated all countries, mixing up fact and fable.
'The orange groves of Sorrento,' he'd whisper, and feel
The strange words spread his soul with sadness.
'The barbarians have descended into the valley,' he'd assert in Latin,
And, as from captivity, his heart would strain towards that valley.
And when his local town, Izyum, was snowed up,
He'd read of how the slavegirls, trampling the grapes with their feet,
Would dance above the vat to the laughter of copper bracelets,
And this would make his throat go dry as last summer.
From the wall his great-grandfather smiled in his cast-iron buckskins
Eternally young, but having lost a lot of lustre.
The glazed December stood like the clock in the dining room,
Looking and waiting, never saying a word.
And then spring, the sloven, in her wet stockings
Came bustling, laughing, and kissed the hollow
At his temples – and the boy would grow speechless from her gibes.
All the lessons – head over heels! All the rules – mixed up!
He ran to look at the river's ice-drift, and the April wind
Blew the clouds as from a bubble-pipe. MARCUS AURELIUS
Waited with classical patience, open at the wrong page.
They were selling pickled apples. The birds and frozen
In the blue-eyed abyss, higher than the bells!
And for this sadness there were already not enough words.
And the hands of the fatherland were touching his hair . . .
He had just reached the age to enlist when it began.
He died, as he'd dreamed he would, in battle, defending the flag.
We'd like to know — why are we treated like this, Lord?
We don't know.

[Small Zone, 2 May 1983]

128

A clumsy saw
(*to Tanya Velikanova*)

A clumsy saw,
Luxuriant sawdust.
Pre-autumn tasks.
May we live until our exile!
Quickly, quickly to the relay point,
Into your warm sweater – quickly,
Freedom's treading on your heels,
Part foul language,
Part searches and part surveillance.
The year '83 –
With salt, no bread –
Will pass with a crunch to the bones,
Will break in two, just about.
They haven't disentangled it.
Beyond the gates, beyond the perimeter –
Higher with each note!
The quiet angel has flown away.
Fate will turn our lives,
If only we can live that long!
Well, until our meeting somewhere.
Zeks' luck –
Smile!
Happy journey.
I've no strength to say goodbye.

[1 September 1983]

So tomorrow, our little ship, Small Zone

So tomorrow, our little ship, Small Zone,
What will come true for us?
According to what law –
Like an eggshell over dead waves?
Covered in patches and scars,
On the word – the honest word – alone –
By whose hand our ship is preserved,
Our little home?
Which of us will sail to the end, row, live to the end –
Let them tell for the others:
We have known
The touch of this river.

[18 September 1983]

To Tanya and Vanya (Osipova and Kovalyov)

I will travel through the land –
With my retinue of guards,
I will study the eyes of human suffering,
I will see what no one has seen –
But will I be able to describe it?
Will I cry how are we able to do this –
Walk on partings as on water?
How we begin to look like our husbands –
Our eyes, foreheads, the corners of our mouths.
How we remember them – down to each last vein of their skins –
They who have been wrenched away from us for years,
How we write to them: 'Never mind,
You and I are one and the same,
Can't be taken apart!'
And, fettered to the ground,
'Forever' sounds in answer –
That most ancient of words
Behind which, without shadow, is the light.
I will tramp out my deportation,
And I will remember everything –
By heart! – they won't be able to take it from me! –
How we breathe –
Each breath outside the law!
What we live by –
Until the morrow.

[12 November 1983]

I will live and survive

I will live and survive and be asked:
How they slammed my head against a trestle,
How I had to freeze at nights,
How my hair started to turn grey . . .
I will smile. And will crack some joke
And brush away the encroaching shadow.
And I will render homage to the dry September
That became my second birth.
And I'll be asked: 'Doesn't it hurt you to remember?'
Not being deceived by my outward flippancy.
But the former names will detonate in my memory –
Magnificent as old cannon.
And I will tell of the best people in all the earth,
The most tender, but also the most invincible,
How they said farewell, how they went to be tortured,
How they waited for letters from their loved ones.
And I'll be asked: what helped us to live
When there were neither letters nor any news – only walls,
And the cold of the cell, and the blather of official lies,
And the sickening promises made in exchange for betrayal.
And I will tell of the first beauty
I saw in captivity.
A frost-covered window! No doors, nor walls,
Nor cell-bars, nor the long-endured pain –
Only a blue radiance on a tiny pane of glass,
A cast pattern – none more beautiful could be dreamt!
The more clearly you looked, the more powerfully dawned
Those brigand forests, campfires and birds!
And how many times there was bitter cold weather
And how many windows sparkled after that one –
But never was it repeated,
That upheaval of rainbow ice!
And anyway, what good would it be to me now,
And what would be the pretext for that festival?
Such a gift can only be received once,
And once is probably enough.

[30 November 1983]

132

I remember an abandoned church

I remember an abandoned church near Moscow:
The door ajar, and the cupola shattered.
And, screening her child with her hand,
The Virgin Mother quietly mourning –
That the boy's feet are bare,
And once again the cold is at hand
That it's so terrible
To let one's dark-eyed child
Walk off across the snows of Russia – forever – no one knows where –
To be crucified by this people, too . . .
Don't throw stones, it isn't necessary!
Must it really happen again and again –
For love, salvation and miracle,
For his open, undaunted gaze –
That here is to be found a Russian Judas,
That the Russian Pilate is reborn?
But among us, who have come in, there's not a cry,
Not a breath – there's a cramp in our throats:
Across her motherly face
Scratched by broken glass
Are the rough letters of obscene graffiti!
And the infant gazes, as though he were watching an execution.
Wait – I will soon come to you!
In your northern December
My face will burn, but I shall tread
The bloodstained Russian road to the end;
But I will ask you – in your power and glory –
What have you done to my Father's house?
And we shall stand before Him, sculptedly
Created according to His likeness,
And He will knock on our accursed temples
With the sense of a common guilt.
How much longer – on crosses and on executioner's blocks
Through the fire of a mother's anxiety –
Must we clean from shame and filth
His desecrated image?
How much longer must we wash the earth clean
Of violence and lies?
Do you hear, O Lord? If you hear –
Give us the strength to serve her.

I sit on the floor

I sit on the floor, leaning against the radiator –
A southerner, no-gooder!
Long shadows stretch from the grating, following the lamp.
It's very cold.
You want to roll yourself into a ball, chicken-style.
Silently I listen to the night,
Tucking my chin between my knees.
A quiet rumble along the pipe:
Maybe they'll send hot water in!
But it's doubtful.
The climate's SHIZO. Mesozoic era.
What will warm us quicker – a firm ode of Derzhavin,
A disfavoured greeting of Martial,
Or Homer's bronze?
Mashka Mouse has filched a rusk
And is nibbling it behind the latrine pail.
A two-inch robber,
The most innocent thief in the world.
Outside the window there's a bustle –
And into our cell bursts –
Fresh from freedom –
The December brigand wind.
The pride of the Helsinki group doesn't sleep –
I can hear them by their breathing.
In the Perm camp the regime's
Infringer doesn't sleep either.
Somewhere in Kiev another, obsessed,
Is twiddling the knob of the radio . . .
And Orion ascends,
Passing from roof to roof.
And the sad tale of Russia
(Maybe we are only dreaming?)
Makes room for Mashka Mouse, and us and the radio set,
On the clean page, not yet begun,
Opening this long winter
On tomorrow.

[16 December 1983]

Let's be sad
(*for Ilyusha*)

Let's be sad about our teaspoonful of love
My far-off friend! About the fact
Our prison terms are endless,
That all the prophets are so stern –
Ah, if only someone would bless us!
My friend, let's be sad about how
I came running in from March;
You were waiting in the doorway.
And took me into that
Good house. And the curtain of the station
Was so delayed that the hastily
Torn-off sprig had time to flower –
And the narrow cupboard of a room floated
Into a shyness the colour of wax.
Let's be sad that we're
Still so profusely young –
But we, who've been born in an alien land,
With our fate of wandering and pride –
Should we seek to borrow a native land?
Like a bell fallen silent
Is the heart's spasm.
How fathomlessly void is all ahead of us!
But even the very longest sadness
Has a single smile at last.

[30 December 1983]

I talk to the mice and the stars

I talk to the mice and the stars,
I've watered the spring onions,
I'll crumble a rusk on the sill for January,
And he will cut a pattern for me on the casement window
In transparent sugar – two wings:
A cold crunch!
And snowflakes flavoured with mint light.
What does a six-winged seraphim
Taste like? Doesn't sadness have a bitter taste of blue?
Doesn't the first circle contradict the heart?
But I know what to answer him:
'Everything's all right, master –
The filigree seal of your hand
Doesn't melt on my lips, and
There is no star more distinguished
Than those white ones on my shoulders.
I'm awarded these Bethlehem
Epaulettes – I thank you.
That you've made them
As for a woman in lace. As long as I'm alive
I'll keep them clean – I promise,
January.' The sparrows cry:
'Vivat!' so the master should not be sad.
And I drink from a cup that has been adorned
With his fretwork. He says: 'Forgive me,
I was afraid I'd put too much sugar in.
God be with you.'

[January 1984]

No, I'm not afraid

No, I'm not afraid: after a year
Of breathing these prison nights
I will survive into the sadness
To name which is escape.

The cockerel will weep freedom for me
And here – knee-deep in mire –
My gardens shed their water
And the northern air blows in draughts.

And how am I to carry to an alien planet
What are almost tears, as though towards home . . .
It isn't true, I *am* afraid, my darling!
But make it look as though you haven't noticed.

To my unknown friend

Above my half of the world
The comets spread their tails.
In my half of the century
Half the world looks me in the eye.
In my hemisphere the wind's blowing,
There are feasts of plague without end.
But a searchlight shines in our faces,
And effaces the touch of death.
And our madness retreats from us,
And our sadnesses pass through us,
And we stand in the midst of our fates,
Setting our shoulders against the plague.
We shall hold it back with our selves,
We shall stride through the nightmare.
It will not get further than us – don't be afraid
On the other side of the globe!

[26 February 1984]

Like Mandelstam's swallow

Like Mandelstam's swallow
Parting falls towards the heart,
Pasternak sends the rain,
And Tsvetayeva – the wind.
So that the Universe's turning may be achieved
Without a false note,
The word is needed – and poets alone
Are answerable for this.
And the peals of spring whirl by
Over Tyutchevian waters,
And autumn's classicism is manifested
Time and time again.
But no one's voice has yet
Touched freedom with a wing,
Nor brought about freedom, *svoboda*,
Even though it's a Russian word.

[25 April (1984?)]

The wind has changed

The wind has changed,
And the new wind is autocratic.
The sky has been raised like a siege
And has taken the suburbs.
Behind the northern wall
The horses have given a peal of snorts,
But the first flood has broken
Through the breach in the eastern gate.
And at once in the smoky downfall
The remains of the towers have vanished,
The crosses and bells.
My city resisted,
It was magnificent and terrible.
It melted in the roaring sky,
Entirely drowned by it.
And later, when above us
The thunderclouds and the waters had closed —
No one knew their triumph
Or sang the praises of that dawn.
And now there will be no peace for them,
They will constantly model someone —
Ever powerless to repeat
Now a hand, now the hem of a garment.

[2 July 1984]

For the cry from the well

For the cry from the well of 'mama!'
For the crucifix torn from the wall,
For the lie of your 'telegrams'
When there's an order for an arrest –
I will dream of you, Russia.
In the accursedness of your victories,
In the anguish of your impotence,
In the nausea of your hangover –
Why does fear break through?
All has been mourned, all have been sung to rest –
Who do you flinch from all of a sudden?
Though you deny it, take refuge in illusion,
Put all the blame on those who have been killed –
I will still come and stand before you
And look into your eyes.

[5 July 1984]

The white-hot blizzard

The white-hot blizzard
Brands us with Russia.
Black rhetoric of craters,
Dark hollows under the snow:
Go away, eyeless woman, go away!
Only how are we to leave each other,
In our infinite whirling,
In our kinship and conflict with her?
And when at last you break loose
From the oppressive tenderness
Of her despotic embraces,
In which to fall asleep is to do so forever:
Your head swims,
As from the first childish drag at a cigarette,
And your lungs are torn to shreds
Like a cheap envelope.
And then, as you wait for everything that
Has emerged alive from her unpeopled cold
To recover from the narcosis --
To know that the angels of Russia
Freeze to death towards morning
Like sparrows in the frost
Falling from their wires into the snow.

[4 August 1984]